SALMON
RECIPES
FROM
ALASKA

CECILIA G. NIBECK

SALMON RECIPES FROM ALASKA
By Cecilia G. Nibeck

P.O. Box 210241
Anchorage, Alaska 99521-0241

ISBN #0-9622117-1-0

Acknowledgements:

Illustrations: Barbara Lavallee, an Alaskan artist represented by Artique, Ltd., 314 G Street, Anchorage

Design: Fineline Graphics, Anchorage

Publishing consultant: Rainforest Publishing, Anchorage

Typist: Dawn Archbold, Anchorage

Printed in U.S.A.

Foreword

I moved to Alaska in 1972. After one season of salmon fishing on Resurrection Bay I had a freezer full of salmon—but only two salmon recipes! My family soon grew tired of salmon loaf and salmon croquettes, so I sent out a request for recipes to family and friends all over the world. This book is the result. Many thanks to all of you for sharing your recipes.

This book is dedicated to "Cougar," our old grey cat who terrorized the neighborhood and ruled our house for 11 years. He was at my side constantly whenever I cooked salmon. He inspired this book's illustrator and filled us with his own special love. He died the week my cookbook went to the printer. I miss him.

Cecilia G. Nibeck

TABLE OF CONTENTS

Fresh salmon

Smoked salmon

Canned salmon

Please use the forms in the back of this book to order "Salmon Recipes from Alaska" and "Alaskan Halibut Recipes."

SALMON SPREAD

1 pound leftover cooked salmon
8 tablespoons butter
1 to 2 teaspoons lemon juice
Dash of hot pepper sauce or cayenne pepper
Salt and pepper to taste

Process or blend all ingredients to the consistency of butter. Add any other herbs that you like. Serve at room temperature. Good with toast or crackers.

SALMON RICE SALAD

2/3 cup water
1/3 cup uncooked rice
1 teaspoon lemon juice
½ teaspoon lemon peel, grated
⅛ teaspoon salt
Dash of ground pepper
1 cup cooked salmon chunks
1 cup frozen peas
2 tablespoons each green pepper and onion, chopped
Salad dressing (recipe follows)
2 tablespoons toasted almonds, slivered
1 teaspoon each parsley and fresh mint, chopped

In a one-quart pan combine water, rice, lemon juice, peel, salt and pepper. Bring to a boil; reduce heat and simmer, covered, for 20 minutes until rice is tender. Add remaining ingredients except almonds, parsley and mint. Heat for 2 minutes. Stir in remaining ingredients. Cool to room temperature. Serves six.

Salad dressing:
Combine 2 tablespoons each olive oil and white wine vinegar, ¼ teaspoon each salt and dry mustard, and ⅛ teaspoon sugar; mix well. Makes ¼ cup.

SALMON SALAD BOAT

2/3 cup water
5 tablespoons butter or margarine
¼ teaspoon salt
2/3 cup all-purpose flour
3 eggs
Fish and carrot salad (recipe follows)

In a 2-quart pan, combine the water, butter and salt. Add flour all at once, remove pan from heat, and beat ingredients with a wire whip until smooth. Beat in eggs, one at a time, until mixture is smooth and glossy. Spoon into a greased 9-inch springform pan. Spread evenly inside pan.

Bake crust in a 400° oven for 40 minutes or until puffed and brown. Turn off oven. Prick with a wooden pick in 10 to 12 places and leave in closed oven for about 10 minutes to dry, then remove pan from oven and cool completely. Remove crust from pan.

If you make the pastry boat a day ahead, cover loosely with foil and store at room temperature. For longer storage, wrap completely in foil and freeze. Thaw completely, then recrisp pastry uncovered in a 400° oven for 10 minutes. (Recrisp even if stored at room temperature.) Cool, then add the salad and garnish.

Chilled fish and carrot salad:
1 pound salmon fillet, cooked
1 cup frozen peas
½ cup green onion, sliced
1 hard boiled egg, chopped
¼ pound cooked shrimp
½ cup mayonnaise
2 tablespoons tomato chili sauce
2 tablespoons lemon juice
1 tablespoon prepared horseradish
½ teaspoon lemon peel, grated
1 cup carrot, shredded
(continued)

2

Combine salmon pieces, peas, green onion, egg and shrimp. Reserve some shrimp for garnish. In a small bowl, stir together mayonnaise, chili sauce, lemon juice, horseradish, and lemon peel. Gently stir into fish mixture; season with salt and pepper. Cover; chill as long as 24 hours.

To serve, arrange shredded carrots in bottom and up the sides of salad boat. Pile fish salad over carrot and garnish with reserved shrimp and 4 to 6 lemon wedges. Serves four.

SALMON AND PASTA SALAD WITH LEMON DILL SAUCE

Salmon and Pasta Salad:
1½ pounds fresh salmon fillet
¼ cup Lemon Dill vinegar
Salt and freshly ground white pepper
4 quarts water
1½ tablespoons salt
¾ pound fresh spinach fettuccine
2/3 cup red onion, diced
½ cup fresh dill, chopped

Lemon Dill Sauce:
1 tablespoon Dijon mustard
½ cup Lemon Dill vinegar
Salt and freshly ground white pepper
1 cup peanut or safflower oil

To prepare Lemon Dill Sauce, whisk together mustard and Lemon Dill vinegar in a small bowl. Season with salt and white pepper. Dribble in oil in a slow stream, continuing to whisk. Adjust seasoning and set aside. Whisk again if necessary before using. Make salad by arranging salmon in a shallow baking dish. Add enough water to half cover salmon. Add Lemon Dill vinegar and season lightly with salt and pepper. Preheat 400° oven, bake until just done, 10 to 12 minutes. Remove from oven and allow to cool to room temperature in its baking liquid.
(continued)

In a large pot, boil 4 quarts water, add salt, stir, and drop in fettuccine. Stir to separate strands, and cook until tender, 3 to 5 minutes. Pour into colander, drain, and rinse thoroughly under cold running water. Shake colander again to remove all excess water, and transfer pasta to a large bowl. Add ½ cup of onion and ¼ cup of dill. Pour half the Lemon Dill Sauce over pasta, season lightly with salt and pepper and toss well. Drain salmon and pat dry. Coarsely flake fish into a bowl. Add remaining onion and dill, ½ cup sauce, salt and pepper, and toss gently. Arrange pasta on serving platter and mound salmon in center. Serves six.

CURRIED SALMON AND FRUIT PLATES

¼ cup each mayonnaise and unflavored yogurt
2 green onions, finely chopped
3 tablespoons chutney
1 clove garlic, minced or pressed
¼ teaspoon curry powder
3 cups salmon, cooked
Lettuce or spinach leaves
Melon slices, orange slices, grapes, pitted and sliced plums or nectarines
½ cup slivered almonds, toasted

Combine the mayonnaise, yogurt, onions, chutney (chop large pieces), garlic, and curry. Cover and chill.

To serve, break fish into large bite-size chunks and mix with the dressing. On each of 4 lettuce- or spinach-lined plates, arrange 2 or 3 slices of melon and orange, a small cluster of grapes, and 1 sliced plum or nectarine. Mound fish on plates and top with almonds. Serves four.

COLD BOILED SALMON WITH SPICE SAUCE

Spice Sauce:
2 cups salmon bouillon (hot; saved from poaching salmon)
½ cup finely minced onion
½ cup minced dill pickle
6 tablespoons minced parsley
2 tablespoons minced chives
2 tablespoons capers
1 teaspoon sugar
½ teaspoon pepper
6 tablespoons tarragon vinegar
¼ cup olive oil (or salad oil)

Poach whole cleaned salmon in court bouillon to cover. Allow 15 minutes per pound. (See Poached Salmon With Dill Sauce for court bouillon recipe.)
Into the hot salmon bouillon, put the rest of the ingredients. Mix well and serve with cold, boiled salmon.

SALMON TERRINE

Salmon fillets (1 pound)
½ pound sole or rockfish fillet, cubed
¼ cup butter
¼ cup shallots or onions, chopped
½ teaspoon tarragon
¼ cup flour
1½ cups Half-and-Half cream
Salt
½ pound shrimp, cooked
3 eggs
Parsley sprigs (optional)
One package Hollandaise sauce

(continued)

5.

In a 10-inch frying pan, melt ¼ cup butter or margarine. Add ¼ cup chopped shallots or onions and ½ teaspoon tarragon; cook, stirring until onions are soft. Blend in ¼ cup all-purpose flour; cook until bubbly. Remove from heat and gradually stir in 1 ¼ cups half-and-half (light cream). Cook, stirring until it boils and thickens. Remove from heat and stir in ½ teaspoon salt, shrimp, white fish pieces, and 3 slightly beaten eggs.

Whirl part of the mixture at a time in a blender until smooth. Pour half the pureed fish into a 6-cup straight-sided deep terrine or a 4½-inch by 8½-inch loaf pan. Arrange the salmon strips, end to end, down center, then spread remaining pureed fish evenly over top. Place pan inside a larger pan (at least 2 inches deep). Pour boiling water 1 inch deep around mold. Bake in a 350° oven for 30 minutes or until firmly set in center. Cool on a rack, then chill well.

Prepare Hollandaise sauce per package instructions.

Cut in thick slices and lift from terrine, supporting with a spatula. Pass Hollandaise to pour over individual servings. Garnish plates with parsley sprigs, if you wish. Serves eight.

PICKLED SALMON

4 fresh salmon fillets
1 cup vinegar
1 cup white wine
1 cup water
¼ teaspoon mace
Several cloves and whole peppers
¼ teaspoon gingerroot
¼ cup fresh horseradish, grated

Boil salmon in strong salt water and remove. Combine vinegar, wine, and water with spices and boil. Remove horseradish when sufficiently boiled. Pour pickle over salmon. Refrigerate. Serves six.

COLD PICKLED SALMON

2 quarts water, or to cover fish
2 tablespoons mixed pickling spices
1 onion, sliced
1 carrot, sliced
2 sprigs parsley
2 teaspoons dill seed
1 tablespoon salt
¾ cup vinegar
4 to 6 pounds fresh salmon, large fillets
Cheesecloth
1 lemon, thinly sliced
3 tablespoons fresh dill, chopped, or 1 tablespoon dried dill
6 tablespoons sugar
1 cucumber, peeled and sliced
1 cup cherry tomatoes
Dill or Yogurt Mayonnaise (recipe follows)

Put water in pan large enough to hold salmon, add pickling spices, 2 onion slices, carrot, parsley, dill seed, salt, and vinegar. Heat to boiling, then simmer gently for 10 minutes. Add fish tied loosely in cheesecloth. Cook gently until fish looks whitish and opaque. It takes about 15 to 20 minutes for the fillets. Lift out fish or pour off liquid and save it. Cool fish enough to handle, then place in shallow glass dish with rest of onion slices, lemon, and dill. Add sugar to pickling liquid and pour over fish. If it doesn't cover fish, heat more water and vinegar (2 parts water, 1 part vinegar) and add to dish. Place plate on top of fish to keep it submerged. Cover and chill for several days.

To serve, cut fish into neat 2-inch pieces. Mound on large platter. Slice carefully but keep slices together and shape of fish intact. Ladle a little pickling liquid over fish to keep it moist and shiny. Decorate platter with sliced cucumbers, cherry tomatoes. Serve with Dill or Yogurt Mayonnaise. Serves four.

(continued)

Dill Mayonnaise:
Season 2½ cups mayonnaise with 2 tablespoons chopped fresh dill or 2 teaspoons dried dill weed and a little lemon juice. Chill.

Yogurt Mayonnaise:
Combine 1 cup each mayonnaise and plain low fat yogurt and season with 2 teaspoons Dijon-style mustard and 2 teaspoons each minced fresh parsley, tarragon, chives, and a few snips Oriental garlic if you have it in your herb garden (looks like chives but has more exotic flavor).

PICKLED SALMON

2 pounds salmon fillets
1 tablespoon salt
2 cups each white vinegar and water
¼ cup salad oil
1½ tablespoons whole mixed pickling spice
1 teaspoon salt
5 small onions, thinly sliced

Cut salmon into chunks and spread in a single layer in a shallow glass baking dish. Sprinkle with 1 tablespoon salt and let stand, uncovered, about 30 minutes. Rinse salmon well and pat dry.

Combine the vinegar, water, salad oil, pickling spice, and 1 teaspoon salt. Bring to boiling, reduce heat, partially cover, and simmer 30 minutes.

Layer salmon chunks and onion slices in a bowl. Pour the boiling hot pickling liquid over salmon, cover loosely, and let cool. Then cover well and refrigerate for at least 24 hours.

Serve salmon and onion slices in stemmed glasses or small bowls. Spoon some marinade over each serving and accompany with buttered dark bread. You can keep salmon for up to a week when stored, covered, in the refrigerator. Serves three.

COOL SALMON BURRITOS

2½ cups water
1 small onion, sliced
3 whole black peppers
1 small bay leaf
1½ teaspoons lemon juice
½ teaspoon salt
4 salmon steaks, about 1 inch thick
Tomato relish (recipe follows)
2 medium-size tomatoes, chopped
1 large green pepper, seeded and chopped
½ cup green onions, sliced
3 tablespoons canned green chiles, chopped
1 tablespoon lemon juice
1 teaspoon salt
About 1 dozen flour tortillas
Lime wedges
Fresh Coriander
About 1 cup each sour cream and guacamole
2 to 3 cups shredded lettuce

In a large frying pan, combine the water, onion, pepper, bay leaf, lemon juice, and salt. Bring to boiling, cover, and simmer 10 minutes. Place salmon in pan, cover, and simmer gently until fish flakes when tested with a fork, about 10 to 12 minutes. Lift salmon from pan with a spatula; cover and chill. Prepare the tomato relish; cover and chill.

To serve, stack and wrap tortillas in foil and heat in a 350° oven for about 15 minutes or until warm. Arrange salmon on a serving plate; garnish with lime and coriander. Place relish, sour cream, guacamole, and lettuce in bowls.

Let everyone assemble his or her own burrito, first spreading a tortilla with sour cream, adding lettuce, chunks of salmon, relish, and guacamole, and then rolling the tortilla around the filling. Serves three.

Tomato Relish:
Combine tomatoes, pepper, green onions, canned green chiles, lemon juice, and salt.

9

SALMON ASPIC

3 pounds fresh salmon fillet
2 tablespoons carrot, minced
2 tablespoons each onion and celery, chopped
A sprig each of thyme and parsley
2 cloves
½ bay leaf
½ lemon, sliced
2 envelopes of gelatin
1 cup water
Dash of cayenne
1 egg and shell
Cheesecloth

Wrap salmon in a clean piece of cheesecloth and put in a kettle with minced carrot, onion and celery, thyme and parsley, cloves, bay leaf and lemon. Pour boiling water over to cover, salt it, and let boil slowly until tender. When it will pierce with a fork, remove from the kettle. Strain the liquid and measure it; if not enough to make 1 quart, add boiling water to make up the amount.

Soak 2 envelopes of gelatin in 1 cup of cold water for 10 minutes and dissolve in the hot stock. Season highly with more salt. Add pepper and a dash of cayenne if needed. Now, add the shell and white of 1 egg; the shell must be broken and the white beaten until frothy. Set on the fire and bring to a boil. Then place where it will be kept warm, but not cooked, for 20 minutes, after which strain through double cheesecloth. The liquid will be clear.

Pour half the liquid into a mold. Put in the refrigerator until it "sets," and then put the salmon on it. This should be cold, with all bones and skin removed. Add slices of hard-boiled eggs and strips of pimento for a garnish, and add just enough of the cold liquid to hold the ingredients on the first layer of jelly. Put into the refrigerator to chill until it is "set" and then add the rest of the jelly. Let stand overnight, after which it will be ready to serve. Serves four.

JELLIED SALMON WITH BROCCOLI AND CAULIFLOWER

1 pound broccoli, separated into florets
1 pound cauliflower, separated into florets
Water
1 tablespoon distilled white vinegar
1 small onion, halved
1 small carrot, sliced
1 small rib celery, sliced
3 or 4 peppercorns
1 or 2 whole allspice
¼ teaspoon salt, 1 bay leaf
½ teaspoon dried dillweed
4 salmon steaks, 1 inch thick
1 envelope unflavored gelatin
Dill sprigs and additional snipped dill
1 pimento, chopped
1 pimento, cut in strips for garnish

Steam broccoli and cauliflower in steamer basket until crisp-tender. Remove and chill. Add vinegar, onion, carrot, celery, peppercorns, allspice, bay leaf, salt and dill to remaining water in skillet; simmer 5 minutes. Add salmon steaks in single layer. Cover and poach 5 to 6 minutes until thickest part of fish is opaque. Drain fish on paper towels and refrigerate. Strain 1½ cups of poaching liquid into a pint measure. Reserve and chill carrots and celery. Discard onion, bay leaf and extra liquid. Taste liquid; season to taste (you may substitute canned chicken broth if flavor is too fishy). Sprinkle gelatin over 3 tablespoons cold water in small saucepan. Add the 1½ cups poaching liquid. Stir over medium heat until gelatin is completely dissolved. Chill mixture until the consistency of unbeaten egg whites. Arrange chilled salmon, broccoli and cauliflower on a shallow serving platter. Arrange chilled carrot and celery slices on salmon; sprinkle with snipped dill and garnish with dill sprigs. Garnish broccoli with pimento strips; sprinkle chopped pimento on cauliflower. Spoon gelatin mixture over fish and vegetables to glaze. Chill 1 to 2 hours until gelatin is firm. Serves four.

11

CHILLED POACHED SALMON

4- to 8-pound whole salmon
2 large onions, sliced
18 whole black peppers
6 whole allspice
½ cup lemon juice
2 bay leaves
1 tablespoon salt
2 cups dry white wine
4 quarts water

Remoulade Sauce:
½ cup oil
¼ cup white wine vinegar
2 tablespoons Dijon mustard
2 tablespoons prepared horseradish
1 tablespoon catsup
½ teaspoon salt
⅛ teaspoon cayenne
1 hard-cooked egg, chopped
1/3 cup each celery and green onion, chopped

Guacomole Sauce:
3 packages frozen avocado dip

Lemon Dill Mayonnaise:
1¼ cups mayonnaise
¾ teaspoon dill weed
1 teaspoon lemon peel, grated

    In your poaching pan or another pan of similar size
and depth, combine onions, black peppers, allspice,
lemon juice, bay leaves, salt, dry white wine and 4
quarts water. Cover and simmer gently 30 minutes to
1 hour.

Place fish on a pan rack and lower it into boiling liquid. Cover pan tightly with lid or foil. Simmer salmon. Allow 10 minutes of cooking time for each 1-inch thickness of fish (measure the thickest portion) or until salmon flakes easily when prodded with a fork. Lift out salmon on rack. Place fish on a serving platter; cool, cover, and chill at least 3 hours. Before serving, pull off skin on top side of salmon. Garnish with lemon wedges, thin slices of cucumber, and watercress sprigs as desired.

These sauces can be used:

Remoulade sauce: Blend salad oil, white wine vinegar, Dijon mustard, prepared horseradish, catsup, salt, cayenne, and hard-cooked egg. Whirl until smooth. Stir in 1/3 cup each finely chopped celery and sliced green onion.

Guacamole Sauce: Thaw frozen dip before serving.

Lemon Dill Mayonnaise: Stir together 1¼ cups of mayonnaise, ¾ teaspoon dill weed and 1 teaspoon grated lemon peel.

POACHED SALMON WITH HORSERADISH SAUCE

2/3 cup lemon juice
1 small onion, sliced
2 teaspoons instant chicken bouillon granules
¼ teaspoon pepper
4 salmon steaks (about 2 pounds)
2 tablespoons butter or margarine
2 tablespoons all-purpose flour
2 tablespoons prepared horseradish
½ teaspoon salt
1½ cups skim milk
2 tablespoons snipped chives
2 teaspoons lemon juice

(continued)

13

Combine 6 cups water, 2/3 cup lemon juice, onion, bouillon, and pepper. Simmer, uncovered, 5 minutes. Add fish; simmer, covered, 5 to 10 minutes. For sauce, melt butter or margarine. Stir in flour, horseradish, and salt. Add milk. Cook and stir until thickened and bubbly. Cook 1 minute more. Remove from heat; stir in chives and the 2 teaspoons lemon juice. Serve sauce over salmon. Garnish. Serves eight.

POACHED SALMON
WITH MUSTARD MAYONNAISE

1 (4-6 pound) whole salmon
2 tablespoons butter
1/3 cup each onion, carrot, celery and green pepper, chopped
2½ quarts water
¼ cup lemon Juice
1 sprig parsley
5 peppercorns
1 bay leaf
2 teaspoons salt
1 envelope unflavored gelatin
Scored cucumber, thinly sliced garnishes: watercress or parsley
Small clusters fresh green or red grapes
Cheesecloth

Mustard Mayonnaise:
2 cups mayonnaise
¼ cup minced parsley
2 tablespoons each minced onion and Dijon mustard
Dash white pepper

Saute onion, celery, carrot and green pepper in butter for 5 minutes. Add water, lemon juice and seasonings; heat to boiling.

(continued)

14

Wrap salmon in cheesecloth leaving long ends on cloth to serve as handles for removing fish from poaching liquid. Immerse salmon into boiling liquid. Cover and simmer gently. Allow 8 to 10 minutes per pound or 10 minutes per thickness of fish. Remove salmon from liquid; gently remove skin while still warm. Strain liquid; cool completely.

Soften gelatin in 2 cups cooled liquid; heat to dissolve gelatin completely. Chill until mixture barely starts to thicken. Spoon gelatin mixture over salmon, using just enough to coat fish completely. Chill.

Decorate salmon with cucumber; spoon thin layer of gelatin over decorations. Chill. Garnish platter with parsley or watercress and fresh grapes. Prepare Mustard Mayonnaise by mixing all ingredients. Serves six.

POACHED SALMON

3 cups dry white wine
3 cups water
1 teaspoon salt
1 onion
1 bunch celery
1 medium carrot, sliced
¼ teaspoon thyme
2 bay leaves
1 teaspoon tarragon
6 peppercorns, crushed
1 (6-pound) salmon
Watercress, parsley or dill sprigs, and lemon slices (for garnish)
3 tablespoons fresh dillweed, chopped
Mayonnaise or Sour Cream Sauce

(continued)

15

Place all the ingredients except the salmon, sauce, and garnishes in a large pot and boil 10 minutes or more. Gently place salmon in pot and reduce heat to a simmer. Simmer 20 minutes. Remove pan from heat and allow salmon to cool in the liquid. Chill. To serve, remove salmon from liquid and place on a platter. Garnish with watercress leaves, small sprigs of parsley or dill, and lemon slices. Add the fresh chopped dillweed to the Mayonnaise or Sour Cream sauce. Serve on the side. Serves eight.

POACHED SALMON WITH SHRIMP SAUCE

1 salmon (about 7 pounds)
8 bay leaves
4 slices onion
2 teaspoons salt
½ teaspoon allspice
1 quart water
Green olives
Bay leaves

Shrimp Sauce:
2 tablespoons butter or margarine
2 tablespoons flour
½ teaspoon salt
½ teaspoon dry mustard
Pinch of cayenne
1½ cups milk or fish stock
1 tablespoon lemon juice
2 tablespoons dry sherry
2 egg yolks
1 can (4½-5 ounces) shrimp

Wrap salmon in cheesecloth; place on rack in fish poacher. Add bay leaves, onion, salt, allspice, and water. Cover; simmer gently, allowing 8 to 10 minutes per pound. Lift out carefully; remove cheesecloth; trim away and discard skin. Place fish on plank or platter; garnish with green olives and bay leaves.
(continued)

Shrimp Sauce:
   Melt butter or margarine in small saucepan; blend in flour, ½ teaspoon salt, mustard, and cayenne. Gradually add milk or stock. Cook over medium heat, stirring constantly, until mixture boils. Remove from heat; add lemon juice and sherry. Stir into beaten egg yolks; return to saucepan. Add shrimp; heat through.

POACHED SALMON WITH DILL SAUCE

Court Bouillon:
1 carrot, sliced
1 onion, sliced
1 stalk celery, sliced
1 large lemon, sliced
1 bay leaf
4 black peppercorns, slightly crushed
2 sprigs fresh parsley
2 teaspoons salt
3 cups water
6 small salmon steaks (about 1 inch thick)

Dill Sauce:
1 cup mayonnaise
1 teaspoon Dijon-style mustard
2 tablespoons fresh dill, chopped or 2 teaspoons, dried
1 tablespoon fresh lemon juice

   Mix the bouillon ingredients in a 10-inch skillet and bring to a boil. Simmer covered for 30 minutes. Remove vegetables, bay leaf and lemon. Cook salmon steaks in bouillon covered for 8 minutes or until salmon flakes easily with a fork. Mix the sauce ingredients in a serving bowl. Remove salmon and serve with sauce. Serves four.

POACHED SALMON STEAKS WITH LIME DRESSING

1 small onion, chopped
1 celery top, chopped
1 bay leaf
1 teaspoon salt
6 salmon steaks, 1 inch thick
½ cup vegetable oil
¼ cup fresh lime juice
¼ teaspoon black pepper
1 lime, sliced thin
1 lemon, sliced thin

Fill a large shallow skillet halfway with water. Add onion, celery, bay leaf and ½ teaspoon salt and bring to a boil. Add salmon; cover and cook over low heat for about 8 minutes. Cook until salmon is opaque in the center. Remove from heat and lift fish from liquid and place on a small platter. In a bowl, whisk oil, lime juice, remaining salt and pepper; pour over salmon and cool to room temperature, then refrigerate 1 hour. Garnish with lemon and lime slices. Serves six.

SALMON CHOWDER

1/3 cup raw potato, diced
1/3 cup tomato, diced
2 tablespoons green pepper, chopped
1 tablespoon butter
½ teaspoon onion, minced
½ cup salmon chunks
1 envelope instant tomato soup
½ cup boiling water
¾ cup milk

In a saucepan combine potato, tomato, green pepper, butter and onion. Cover and simmer 15-20 minutes or until vegetables are tender. Add water to soup mix and mix well. Gradually add milk to vegetables. Blend in soup mix. Stir in salmon. Heat to serving temperature. Serves two.

SALMON CHOWDER

2 slices bacon
1 large onion, chopped
1 clove garlic, minced
2¼ cups water
½ cup white wine
1 bay leaf
2 whole allspice
3 chicken bouillon cubes
1 salmon steak, 1 inch thick
1 halibut steak, 1 inch thick
¼ cup all-purpose flour
2 cups milk
Nutmeg
Salt and pepper to taste

In a 4-quart or larger pan, cook bacon, diced, over medium heat until crisp. With a slotted spoon, lift out bacon. Remove and discard all but 2 tablespoons drippings from pan. Add onion and garlic; cook, stirring occasionally, until limp. Add 2 cups water, wine, bay leaf, allspice, and bouillon cubes; bring to boiling, cover and simmer 20 minutes. Add salmon and halibut. Cover and simmer until fish flakes, about 10 minutes for fresh fish, 20 minutes for frozen fish. With a slotted spoon, lift fish out. Remove and discard skin and bones; coarsely flake fish and set aside. Mix flour and ¼ cup water until smooth; gradually stir into soup. Cook over medium heat, stirring constantly, until soup thickens. Stir in milk. Return bacon and fish to soup. Cook uncovered, stirring frequently, until soup is hot. Add a dash of nutmeg and salt and pepper to taste. Remove and discard bay leaf and allspice before serving. Garnish with chopped parsley, if desired. Serves four.

SALMON SOUP

1 quart clam juice
¼ cup butter
1/3 cup flour
1 cup cream
½ cup creme fraiche (see note)
1 tablespoon tomato paste
½ pound fresh salmon, cubed
1 medium tomato, peeled and cubed
¼ cup fresh basil
1 tablespoon chopped chives
3 to 6 croutons
Salt and pepper

Bring clam juice to a boil. Make a paste by melting butter and combining with flour. Cook over low heat while stirring for 5 minutes. Add paste to clam juice and bring back to a boil. Stir and reduce heat; simmer 10-15 minutes. Next combine cream, creme fraiche and tomato paste. Add several teaspoons of hot clam juice and stir; then add mixture to remaining clam juice. Salt and pepper to taste. Add salmon chunks, tomatoes and basil to soup. Reheat soup for 5 minutes—do not boil. Ladle soup; add croutons and chives.

NOTE: The creme fraiche is made by combining one cup of cream with one tablespoon buttermilk. Leave covered at room temperature until thickened—about 24 hours.

SALMON STEW

4 slices bacon, cut into 2-inch pieces
1 large onion, chopped
2 large potatoes, diced
1 large can (28 ounces) tomatoes
1 cup dry vermouth (or ¼ cup lemon juice plus ¾ cup water)
1 tablespoon Worcestershire sauce
4 whole bay leaves
2 or 3 cloves garlic, minced or pressed
2 teaspoons salt
½ teaspoon pepper
2 pounds salmon fillets cut into 2-inch pieces

In a 4- or 5-quart pan, fry bacon over medium heat until browned; add onion and potatoes to bacon and drippings and cook, stirring, for 10 minutes, or until onion is limp. Add tomatoes and their liquid and break up tomatoes with a spoon. Stir In vermouth, Worcestershire, bay leaves, garlic, salt, and pepper; cover and simmer for 30 minutes or until potatoes are tender. Add salmon, stirring gently to mix; cover and continue cooking for 5 minutes or until fish flakes easily with a fork. Serves four to five.

BARBECUED SALMON STEAKS

4 salmon steaks, ¾ inch thick
¼ cup butter, melted
1½ teaspoons soy sauce
1 tablespoon lemon juice
1 garlic clove, crushed
1 tablespoon Worcestershire sauce
Dash Tabasco

Combine ingredients; mix well. Brush steaks with mixture. Place steaks on oiled grill over hot coals; grill 10 minutes or until salmon flakes with fork. Turn salmon halfway. Baste frequently and once after salmon is removed from the grill. Serves four.

BARBECUED SALMON

¼ cup olive oil
¼ cup butter
¼ cup lemon or lime juice
1 large clove garlic, minced
¼ teaspoon each salt and pepper
¼ teaspoon Worcestershire sauce
¼ teaspoon thyme or tarragon, crushed
⅛ teaspoon cayenne pepper
6 salmon steaks

Combine all ingredients except steaks; mix well. Brush mixture on both sides of steaks. Grill steaks over charcoal, allowing 10 minutes per inch of thickness of salmon. Brush steaks frequently with sauce, turning steaks once during cooking. Before removing steaks from cooking grill, brush steaks thoroughly. Serves six.

SALMON GRILLED IN LETTUCE

1/3 cup lemon juice
1/3 cup olive oil
3 tablespoons fresh parsley, chopped
3 tablespoons green onions, minced
½ teaspoon fennel seeds
6 salmon steaks, 1 inch thick
12 dark green romaine lettuce leaves
1 ½ tablespoons vegetable oil
3 tablespoons wet tea leaves

Mix lemon juice, olive oil, 2 tablespoons of parsley, 2 tablespoons of onions, and fennel seeds in a pie plate. Add salmon and coat. Marinate for 1 hour at room temperature, turning several times. Cut 12 pieces of twine. Lay 1 piece of twine crosswise with another on the table. Place 1 lettuce leaf over twine, add salmon and some marinade; sprinkle with some fennel seeds, parsley, and onions. Cover with another lettuce leaf, fold lettuce around salmon and tie strings. Brush packet with oil. For outdoor grilling: Sprinkle tea leaves on coals and place packets on grill about 5 inches from coals. Cook covered for 16 minutes, turning after 8 minutes. Test doneness by removing salmon and looking at the center of the salmon to see if it is opaque and flakes easily. If not done, refold packet and return to heat for 3-5 minutes. For indoor cooking: Use broiler at 450° and place salmon packets in shallow pan. Cook 6 minutes per side. Test for doneness. Serves six.

BULGUR STUFFED SALMON STEAKS

4 salmon steaks, 1 inch thick
½ cup bulgur wheat
2 tablespoons lemon juice
2 tablespoons butter, melted
2 tablespoons parsley, snipped
1 tablespoon green onion, sliced
½ teaspoon ground coriander
¼ teaspoon salt
Hickory chips
Cooking oil
Brown sugar
Aluminum foil

In a small bowl cover bulgur with 1 inch boiling water and let stand 30 minutes; drain. Combine lemon juice and butter; set aside. Stir bulgur, parsley, onions, coriander and salt. Form a 12-inch by 8-inch pan out of aluminum foil; brush with oil. Place salmon in pan; brush with lemon mixture. Spoon ¼ of the stuffing into the salmon cavity. Soak hickory chips and prepare charcoal in a covered grill. Arrange the coals around the edge of the grill; sprinkle hickory chips over the coals. Place pan on the grill; cover with hood for 25 minutes. Sprinkle brown sugar over salmon; cook, covered, 5 minutes longer. Remove and sprinkle with more sugar. Serves four.

GRILLED SALMON STEAKS
WITH ANCHOVY BUTTER

¼ pound (1 stick) unsalted butter, softened
4 8-ounce slices fresh salmon steak
1 teaspoon tarragon
Salt
Freshly ground black pepper
1 tablespoon anchovy paste

Melt 2 tablespoons of butter and add tarragon to it. Brush salmon steaks with half the melted butter, then sprinkle very lightly with salt and pepper. Place in a preheated broiler and broil until one side is golden brown. Turn the fish, brush with remaining butter, and broil second side until it is golden brown and fish flakes easily when tested with fork.

Make anchovy butter by creaming together the remaining softened butter with the anchovy paste. Remove salmon steaks to a warm platter and top each piece with anchovy butter. Serves four.

GRILLED FRESH SALMON

½ cup melted butter or margarine
1/3 cup lemon juice
1 large clove of garlic, sliced
6 pounds salmon fillets

Combine butter or margarine, lemon juice, and garlic. Place salmon fillets in oiled flat wire broiling basket with long handle. Brush flesh side with butter sauce. Grill over charcoal coals flesh-side down about 10 minutes or until lightly brown, brushing with sauce occasionally. Turn salmon; brush side with sauce; place a piece of foil loosely on top. Continue broiling 10 to 15 minutes or until just done. Throw garlic chips on charcoal last 5 minutes to get full benefit of garlic. Serves eight.

GRILLED SALMON STEAKS WITH MUSTARD SAUCE

4 salmon steaks, each about 1 inch thick
Olive oil or salad oil
¼ cup each dry white wine and whipping cream
1 tablespoon Dijon mustard
2 tablespoons butter or margarine
Salt and pepper

Wipe fish with a damp cloth; brush each side with oil. Place salmon steaks on a well-greased grill 4 to 6 inches above a solid bed of medium-glowing coals. Cook, turning once, for 5 to 8 minutes on each side or until fish flakes easily when prodded with a fork. Transfer to a warm serving platter; keep warm.

In a small pan, combine the wine, cream, and mustard. Bring mixture to a boil and boil rapidly until volume is reduced to about ¼ cup. Remove from heat; with a wire whip or wooden spoon, beat in butter until sauce is thickened and creamy. Season with salt and pepper. Spoon sauce over fish. Serves four.

GRILLED SALMON AND VEGETABLES

4 salmon steaks cut in 1-inch chunks
4 to 6 small zucchini, cut in 1-inch lengths
2 to 3 small onions, peeled and cut in ½-inch-thick slices
2 to 3 small green peppers, cut in 1-inch-wide strips
1½ to 2 dozen medium-sized mushrooms
1 small eggplant, cut in 1-inch chunks

Soy-Sherry baste:
2 cups soy sauce
2 cups dry sherry or chicken broth
2 tablespoons salad oil

(continued)

26

Stir together 2 cups each soy sauce and dry sherry (or regular strength chicken broth) and 2 tablespoons salad oil. Pour into individual bowls at least 3 inches deep. You can pour any remaining sauce into a small pitcher and set it on the table to replenish bowls as needed.

Arrange salmon and vegetables on skewer and baste often. Cook over medium-hot coals. Serves four.

SALMON AND SCALLOP BROCHETTES

1 pound whole sea scallops
1½ pounds fillet of salmon, cut equal to size of scallops
Olive oil
1 pound sweet butter at room temperature
2 large bunches basil, chopped
Lemon juice to taste

Beat butter and basil together with wooden spoon by hand to prevent oxidation of basil which would make it darken. Serve butter at warmer than refrigerator temperature so that it melts evenly.

Arrange scallops and salmon squares alternately onto skewers. Pieces should be close together but not too tight. Brush them lightly with olive oil and place on a very hot hibachi grill for 3 to 4 minutes on the first side, 2 minutes on the second, turning only once. After turning, brush with olive oil once. Be careful not to drip oil onto coals as it might flare up. Serve brochettes with basil butter. Serves eight.

27

BARBECUED SALMON STEAKS WITH PARMESAN-TOPPED VEGETABLES

6 salmon steaks, 1 inch thick
6 to 8 small whole red-skinned new potatoes, precooked
4 medium-sized zucchini, precooked and cut into 2-inch pieces
½ cup melted butter or margarine
Lemon wedges
¼ cup each grated Parmesan cheese and finely chopped parsley

Lemon Herb Dressing:
1/3 cup lemon juice
½ cup each olive oil and salad oil
1 teaspoon each sugar, salt, dry mustard and Italian seasoning
¼ teaspoon pepper
1 clove garlic, pressed
1 tablespoon instant minced onion

Combine Lemon Herb Dressing ingredients together and shake to blend. Marinate fish steaks with dressing in refrigerator overnight. Turn once.

To barbecue, arrange a well-greased grill 6 inches above a bed of low-glowing coals. Thread potatoes and zucchini on separate skewers. Generously brush fish and vegetables with melted butter.

Arrange vegetables on one side of grill, salmon steaks on other side. Cook vegetables, turning frequently, until browned on all sides. Cook fish, basting with butter and turning once with a spatula, until it flakes when probed with fork, 8 to 10 minutes on each side. Transfer fish to serving platter; garnish with lemon wedges to squeeze over. Arrange vegetables in a shallow casserole; toss with remaining butter, cheese, and parsley. Serves six.

SALMON SUPREME

1 (5- to 8-pound) whole, dressed salmon
Salt and pepper
2 tablespoons butter or margarine, softened
½ medium onion, sliced
½ lemon, sliced
2 or 3 sprigs fresh parsley
Oil
Lemon wedges

Wash salmon and pat dry. Sprinkle inside of fish with salt and pepper; dot with butter. Arrange overlapping slices of onion, lemon and parsley in cavity. Brush salmon with oil. Wrap in heavy-duty aluminum foil; seal edges with double fold. Place on grill over medium-hot coals. Carefully turn salmon every 10 minutes. Cook until fish flakes easily. Transfer salmon to serving platter and fold back foil. Cut between bone and meat with wide spatula; lift off each serving. Serve with lemon wedges. Serves eight.

GRILLED SALMON

4 salmon fillets, about 1 inch thick
1 cup olive oil
Basil leaf stems

Basil Sauce:
2 cups fresh basil leaves, stems reserved for marinade for salmon
1 cup olive oil
2 tablespoons minced garlic (about 4 to 5 large cloves)
¼ cup pine nuts
Salt

(continued)

Marinate salmon fillets in a glass bowl with olive oil mixed with basil leaf stems in refrigerator for at least 2 hours.

Grill salmon over very hot coals for 3 to 4 minutes to a side, until firm. Serve immediately with 2 tablespoons Basil Sauce on top of each fillet. Pound basil leaves using a mortar and pestle. Slowly add olive oil and stir until mixture becomes paste-like. Add minced garlic and blend well. Stir in pine nuts and add salt to taste. Serves four.

MARINATED ORANGE SALMON STEAKS

4 salmon steaks, 1 inch thick
1/3 cup orange juice
1/3 cup soy sauce
2 tablespoons snipped parsley
2 tablespoons cooking oil
1 clove garlic, crushed
½ teaspoon dried basil, crushed

Place fish in a shallow dish. Combine orange juice, soy sauce, parsley, oil, garlic, and basil; pour over fish. Let stand at room temperature for 2 hours turning the steaks occasionally. Drain, reserving marinade. Place fish directly on grill. Grill over medium-hot coals about 8 minutes or until fish is light brown. Baste with marinade and turn. Grill 8 to 10 minutes more or until fish flakes easily when tested with a fork. Meanwhile, heat remaining marinade to boiling. Transfer fish to serving platter. Serves four.

BARBECUE SMOKED SALMON

6 salmon fillets, 1 to 1½ inches thick
1 tablespoon chopped parsley
½ teaspoon each dill weed and sugar
¼ teaspoon salt
1 clove garlic, pressed
½ teaspoon grated lemon peel
2 cups hickory chips
Water
Salad oil

Cut fillets into 2-inch-wide strips. Mix together the parsley, dill, sugar, salt, garlic, and lemon peel; rub evenly over the fish. Cover and let stand at room temperature while you prepare the fire.

When you ignite the charcoal, also immerse hickory chips in water for about 30 minutes, then drain well. Spread the coals out slightly and scatter the drained hickory chips directly on top. Set the greased grill in place 4 to 6 inches above coals and immediately lay the fish pieces, slightly apart, on the grill. Cover the barbecue and adjust the top and bottom dampers so they are open just a crack.

Let fish cook slowly for about 20 minutes before testing for doneness; when done, the fish should flake easily when prodded with a fork. Lift with a wide spatula and transfer to a warm serving platter. Serves six.

SALMON STEAKS
WITH BROCCOLI SAUCE

4 salmon steaks
4 teaspoons margarine
½ cup chicken broth
2 tablespoons lemon juice
1 cup broccoli
¼ cup minced onion
1 clove garlic, minced
¼ teaspoon salt
⅛ teaspoon pepper

Preheat oven to 375°. Arrange salmon steaks in shallow baking dish. Dot evenly with margarine. Sprinkle with 1 tablespoon of lemon juice. Bake 20 minutes or until fish flakes easily with fork. Break broccoli into small pieces and cook in chicken broth with onion and garlic until broccoli is tender. Pour into blender with 1 tablespoon of lemon juice and salt and pepper. Blend until smooth. Serve over cooked salmon.

CURRY SALMON STEAKS

6 salmon steaks, 1½ inches thick
½ cup sherry wine
½ cup chicken broth
Salt and pepper

Sauce:
1 shallot, chopped
1 teaspoon flour
1 teaspoon curry powder
2 egg yolks
½ cup of cream
1 pint chicken broth

(continued)

Place salmon steaks in a flat, oiled pan. Season with salt, pepper, wine and broth. Cover with pepperoil and cook in oven at 350° for 20 minutes. Place fish on hot platter and keep hot. Cover with sauce.

Saute chopped shallot with 1 teaspoon flour and 1 teaspoon curry powder and heat through. Add broth in which fish was cooked, and 1 pint of broth. Boil for 10 minutes. Blend with the yolks of 2 eggs and ½ cup of cream. Strain and pour over fish. Serves six.

BROILED SALMON STEAKS

4 salmon steaks, 1 inch thick
1 small onion, chopped
3 tablespoons butter
3 tablespoons parsley, minced
3 tablespoons cognac
1/3 cup dry wine
2 cups bread crumbs
¼ cup butter, melted
2 tablespoons lemon juice

Melt butter and saute onion in a skillet until tender. Add parsley, cognac and wine. Simmer uncovered 15 minutes or until liquid is absorbed. Stir in soft crumbs and stir over low heat until crumbly. Next, brush salmon with a mixture of butter and lemon juice. Place salmon butter side up on a broiler pan and broil for 5 minutes. Turn salmon and spread crumb mixture on top; broil 5-6 minutes until topping is golden brown and crisp. Garnish with sprigs of fresh dill. Serves four.

SALMON WITH CAVIAR SAUCE

2 cups hot water
1 cup white wine
1 small onion, sliced
¼ cup celery, sliced
6 peppercorns
1 bay leaf
1¼ teaspoons salt
2 pounds salmon steaks
1 envelope unflavored gelatin
¼ cup cold water
Caviar dressing (recipe follows)

Combine hot water, ¾ cup wine, vegetables, peppercorns, bay leaf and salt in deep skillet. Bring to boil, reduce heat, cover and simmer 15 minutes. Add salmon; return to boil, reduce heat, cover and simmer 10-15 minutes. Remove from heat and cool 30 minutes. Lift salmon to flat platter and chill for 2 hours. Drain stock through several layers of cheesecloth; measure 1 cup. Add remaining wine. Soften gelatin in ¼ cup cold water in custard cup 5 minutes. Heat cup in pan of simmering water until gelatin dissolves. Stir in stock. Chill until liquid is consistency of unbeaten egg whites. Transfer salmon to wire rack; brush with gelatin glaze several times. Chill 15 minutes; continue to glaze until well coated. Refrigerate 1 hour. Serve on platter garnished with parsley and lemon wedges; include caviar dressing. Serves four.

Caviar Dressing:
½ cup mayonnaise
½ cup sour cream
1 tablespoon lime juice
1 teaspoon grated lime peel
2 tablespoons black caviar, rinsed and drained

Combine mayonnaise, sour cream, lime juice and grated lime peel in small bowl. Just before serving, fold in caviar. Parsley and onion may be used instead of caviar. Makes 1 cup.

SALMON AND VEGETABLES

1½ pounds salmon fillet, skinned
1 cup sauterne
1 small onion, chopped
2 sprigs parsley
1 bay leaf
Salt
2 10-ounce packages of frozen spinach
1 cup carrots cut in julienne strips
1 cup celery cut in julienne strips
1½ cups cream
4 teaspoons cornstarch
¼ teaspoon ground nutmeg
Dash paprika

Cut salmon into 4 pieces and place in skillet. Add sauterne, onion, parsley, bay leaf and ¼ teaspoon salt. Bring to boil, reduce heat, cover and simmer 5-8 minutes. Follow package instructions and cook spinach. Drain and keep warm. Cook carrots and celery in boiling water 8-10 minutes. Drain and keep warm. Remove salmon from skillet and strain salmon cooking liquid. Boil liquid until ½ cup remains. Combine cream, cornstarch, nutmeg, paprika and ⅛ teaspoon salt; stir into skillet. Bring to a boil and cook 2 minutes longer. Spread spinach on dishes. Arrange salmon, carrots and celery atop; drizzle sauce over salmon. Serves four.

SALMON CAPER BROIL

2 tablespoons butter
1 tablespoon capers, chopped
1 tablespoon snipped parsley
4 salmon steaks

Stir together butter, capers and parsley. Place salmon on greased, unheated rack of broiler pan; spread half of the butter mixture over the salmon. Broil 4 inches from heat for 7 minutes; turn and spread remaining butter mixture over salmon. Broil 4 minutes more or until salmon flakes. Serves four.

ORIENTAL MARINATED SALMON

Equal parts, depending upon the amount of salmon:
Teriyaki sauce
Vermouth
Italian dressing

Mix ingredients and marinate salmon in it until ready to cook. Baste with the sauce while baking or grilling. Heat sauce and pour over cooked salmon when serving.

ORIENTAL SALMON KABOBS

1/3 cup soy sauce
¼ cup oil
2 tablespoons green onion, minced
2 tablespoons sugar
1 clove garlic, minced
2 tablespoons sesame seeds
1 small onion, quartered
1 pound salmon, chunked
2 cups broccoli
8-10 medium mushrooms

Combine soy sauce, oil, green onion, sugar, garlic and sesame seeds; mix well. Marinate salmon 30 minutes. Alternate onion slices, salmon, broccoli and mushrooms on each of 4 long-handled skewers. Brush with marinade. Place on cooking grid of covered cooker over medium-hot charcoal briquets 10-12 minutes; turn and baste every 2 or 3 minutes. Serves four.

ORIENTAL SALMON KABOBS

1¼ pounds salmon, chunked
1 large cucumber, peeled and cut in ¾-inch slices
¼ cup soy sauce
¼ cup dry sherry
1 tablespoon white wine vinegar
2 teaspoons honey
1 teaspoon ginger root, grated
1 clove garlic, minced
1 teaspoon cornstarch
Rice steamed with 2 tablespoons sliced green onion and 1 tablespoon sesame seeds

(continued)

37

Combine soy sauce, sherry, vinegar, honey, ginger and garlic; pour over salmon and cucumbers. Marinate ½ hour. Alternate salmon and cucumbers on skewers. Broil or barbecue 5 inches from heat, 1 minute on each of 4 sides or until salmon flakes easily with a fork. Baste with marinade each time turned. Stir cornstarch into remaining marinade; heat and stir until slightly thickened. Serve with sesame rice. Serves four.

GOLDEN BROILED SALMON

1 cup mushrooms, sliced
1 medium onion, sliced
4 salmon fillets
3 egg yolks
1 cup vegetable oil
Salt and white pepper
Aluminum foil

Saute onions and mushrooms in a little oil until limp. Cut 4 12-inch squares of aluminum foil and oil the tops. Scatter onions and mushrooms in the middle of each foil square and place a salmon fillet on top, skin side down. Whip egg yolks and 1 cup oil until foamy. Add salt and pepper. Spoon sauce over the fillets. Fold and seal the packets securely and place in baking pan. Bake 10-15 minutes at 550°. Place packets on plates for guests to open. Add lemon wedges. Serves four.

PAN-GRILLED SALMON STEAKS

8 salmon steaks, 1 inch thick
3 tablespoons unsalted butter, melted
Salt and black pepper
Lemon wedges

Brush salmon with melted butter and season with salt and pepper. Place salmon on preheated broiler pan and broil 5 minutes per side. Remove from pan and place on a heated platter; garnish with lemon wedges. Serves eight.

SALMON FILLETS
WITH APPLE BUTTER

4 8-ounce salmon fillets
4 tablespoons unsalted butter
4 cups onions, sliced thin
Salt and pepper to taste
½ cup apple butter

Using a pair of needle-nosed pliers or tweezers, remove the floating ribs from the salmon. You will find these bones by running your fingers along the side of the fish and pulling them out like splinters. Remove the skin. Melt the butter over low heat in an ovenproof skillet. Slowly stew the onions until they have cooked without coloring. Add salt and pepper to taste. Place the fillets on the onions and spread each with 2 tablespoons of the apple butter. Bake in a preheated 375° oven 20-25 minutes, or until the salmon flakes easily with a fork. Serve immediately, placing a fillet of salmon onto each plate on its bed of onions. Serves four.

FISH STEAKS MINCEUR

¾ cup water
¾ cup dry white wine
1 teaspoon dried leaf thyme
1 bay leaf
¼ teaspoon Tabasco pepper sauce
1 large carrot, cut in julienne strips
1 zucchini, cut in julienne strips
1 red pepper, cut in julienne strips
1 leek (white portion only), cut in julienne strips
4 salmon steaks, 1 inch thick
1 egg yolk

In large skillet combine water, wine, thyme, bay leaf and Tabasco sauce; bring to boil. Add carrot, zucchini, red pepper and leek. Arrange fish steaks on top of vegetables. Reduce heat, cover and simmer 10-12 minutes until fish flakes easily with a fork. Transfer fish steaks to heated serving platter. Remove vegetables from skillet and reserve. Reduce poaching liquid to ¾ cup. Remove bay leaf. Strain; pour into container of electric blender. Add 1 cup reserved vegetables and egg yolk, cover and process until smooth. Spoon sauce around fish steaks on serving platter. Arrange remaining vegetables on top of fish. Serves four.

BROILED SALMON

Arrange 4 salmon steaks or fillets on lightly greased broiler pan. If desired, brush with glaze (below). Broil 5-6 inches from heat 8-10 minutes on each side or until fish flakes easily, brushing occasionally with remaining glaze. Spoon any leftover glaze over fish on serving plate. Season with salt and pepper. Serves four.

Tangy Glaze:
In small saucepan, combine ¼ cup butter, ¼ cup firmly packed brown sugar and 2 tablespoons lemon juice. Heat to melt butter and combine ingredients.

(continued)

Dill Glaze:
Same as Tangy Glaze, except omit brown sugar and add ¾ teaspoon dill weed.

Lemon Glaze:
Same as Tangy Glaze, except omit brown sugar.

SALMON WITH DILL SAUCE

4 salmon steaks or fillets
1 teaspoon salt
1 medium onion, sliced
1 cube or 1 teaspoon chicken bouillon
1½ cups water
1 tablespoon lemon juice
Dill Sauce (recipe follows)

In large skillet, large enough to hold fish in a single layer, combine salt, onion, chicken bouillon, water and lemon juice. Heat to boiling. Add salmon steaks, simmer tightly covered for 10 minutes or until fish flakes easily. Remove salmon to platter; pour Dill Sauce over salmon and serve. Serves four.

Dill Sauce:
2 tablespoons margarine or butter
1 tablespoon finely chopped onion
2 tablespoons flour
1 teaspoon salt
1 teaspoon dill weed
⅛ teaspoon pepper
1½ cups milk

In small saucepan, cook onion in margarine until tender; stir in flour, salt, dill weed and pepper. Add milk, mixing well. Heat until mixture boils and thickens, stirring constantly.

41

SALMON STEAKS BERNAISE

4 salmon steaks, ½-inch thick
4 small red potatoes
Salt
Water
¼ cup white wine vinegar
1 tablespoon minced green onion
1½ teaspoons tarragon
¼ teaspoon pepper
2 egg yolks
¾ cup butter or margarine
1 tablespoon parsley, chopped
Salad oil
1/3 cup sour cream
4 large pitted ripe olives, minced
Watercress for garnish

In 1-quart saucepan over high heat, heat unpeeled potatoes, ½ teaspoon salt, and enough water to cover to boiling. Reduce heat to medium-low; cover and cook 10 to 15 minutes until potatoes are fork-tender. Drain potatoes; keep warm.

Meanwhile, prepare Bearnaise Sauce: In double boiler top, combine vinegar, green onion, tarragon, and pepper; over high heat, heat to boiling. Boil about 3 minutes or until vinegar is reduced to about 1 tablespoon. Place double-boiler top over double-boiler bottom with hot, not boiling, water. Add egg yolks and cook, beating constantly with wire whisk until slightly thickened. Add butter or margarine, a tablespoon at a time, beating constantly with wire whisk until butter is melted and mixture is thickened. Stir in parsley. Keep sauce warm.

(continued)

Preheat broiler. Lightly brush rack in broiling pan with salad oil. Place salmon steaks on rack; lightly sprinkle with salt. Broil 3 minutes. Turn salmon steaks; broil 2 minutes longer. To serve, cut each potato in half. Spoon a dollop of sour cream on each potato half; top with some minced ripe olives. Arrange salmon steaks and potatoes on warm platter; garnish with watercress. Pass Bearnaise Sauce in small bowl. Serves four.

SALMON WITH ALMONDS AND PECANS

1½ pounds salmon fillet, skinned and sliced crossways into 8 portions
3 tablespoons all-purpose flour
2 tablespoons butter or margarine
1/3 cup sliced almonds
1/3 cup pecan halves
¼ cup dry white wine

White butter sauce:
½ cup dry white wine
1 shallot or onion, chopped
1 teaspoon tarragon, crushed, or 3 teaspoons fresh tarragon
¼ cup whipping cream
¾ cup unsalted butter
4 teaspoons lemon juice
¼ teaspoon salt
⅛ teaspoon white pepper
2 tablespoons snipped chives

(continued)

43

Dip salmon slices into flour, turning to coat lightly. In a large skillet, melt first 2 tablespoons butter. Cook salmon in hot butter over medium heat for 4 to 5 minutes on each side or until fish flakes easily when tested with a fork. Remove salmon from skillet; keep warm.

Add remaining 2 tablespoons butter to skillet. Add almonds and pecans; cook and stir over medium heat about 3 minutes or just until nuts are brown; remove nuts. Add wine to skillet. Bring to boil; cook and stir over medium heat for 2 to 3 minutes, scraping up any browned bits from bottom of skillet. Add white butter sauce and heat through but do not boil. Return nuts to skillet; stir in chives. To serve, arrange 2 salmon slices on each of 4 plates. Spoon sauce over salmon. Serves four.

White butter sauce:
In a medium saucepan, combine wine, shallot, fresh tarragon or dried tarragon. Simmer over medium heat about 4 minutes or until liquid is reduced to 1/3 cup. Stir in whipping cream. Continue cooking until mixture measures 1/3 cup. Reduce heat. Cut unsalted butter into small pieces. Using a wire whisk, whip butter into mixture, one piece at a time. Do not boil. Stir in lemon juice, salt, and white pepper. Strain. Makes 1 cup.

CORN MEAL SALMON STEAKS

4 salmon steaks, 1 inch thick
1½ teaspoons salt
⅛ teaspoon freshly ground black pepper
½ cup corn meal
1½ tablespoons butter or margarine
1½ tablespoons cooking oil
4 large lemon wedges

Sprinkle each side of each steak with salt and pepper; spread corn meal out on a piece of waxed paper and press steaks gently into meal so that they are lightly dredged on each side. Brown the steaks lightly on one side, then on the flip side, in the butter and oil in a very large heavy skillet set over moderately high heat. As soon as the steaks are browned, reduce heat to low, cover skillet and cook 12 to 15 minutes or until a steak, gently probed with a fork, will flake. Serve with large wedges of lemon. Serves four.

PAN-FRIED SALMON

4 salmon fillets
1 tablespoon lemon juice
¼ cup flour
1 teaspoon salt
¼ teaspoon white pepper
3 tablespoons corn oil

Wash and dry the salmon. Sprinkle with the lemon juice and dip in a mixture of the flour, salt and pepper. Heat the oil in a skillet; saute the salmon until browned on both sides. Serve with tartar sauce if desired. Serves four.

SALMON ORIENTAL

2 salmon steaks, 1 inch thick
2 teaspoons salt
¼ teaspoon pepper
¼ cup flour
4 tablespoons butter
2 cups onions, sliced
1 cup green pepper, chopped
3 stalks celery, chopped
2 tablespoons cornstarch
2 cups chicken broth
1 cup canned corn
2 tablespoons soy sauce
1 teaspoon sugar
1 pound spaghetti, cooked and drained

Cut the salmon into 2-inch cubes, discarding the skin and bones. Dip the cubes in a mixture of the salt, pepper, and flour, coating all sides. Melt the butter in a skillet. Add salmon and brown lightly on all sides. Remove salmon. In the butter remaining, saute the onions, green pepper, and celery 10 minutes. Mix cornstarch and broth until smooth. Add to skillet, stirring constantly to the boiling point, then cook over low heat 5 minutes. Add the corn, soy sauce, and sugar. Cook 1 minute. Taste for seasoning.

Spread the spaghetti in a buttered casserole and arrange the salmon over it. Pour sauce over all. Cover the casserole. Bake in a 350° oven for 30 minutes, removing the cover for the last 5 minutes. Serves four.

SALMON AND TOMATO SAUCE

6 salmon fillets, 1 inch thick
4 tablespoons olive oil
1 small onion
1 8-ounce can tomato sauce
2/3 cup water
¼ teaspoon basil
½ teaspoon oregano
¼ teaspoon sugar

Saute salmon fillets in 2 tablespoons olive oil. Place in baking dish. Saute onion in 2 tablespoons olive oil. When light brown, add tomato sauce and water. Cook for 15 minutes. Add basil, oregano, and sugar, and cook for 5 more minutes. Pour onion mixture over salmon. Bake in 350° oven for 20 minutes. Serves four.

HAWAIIAN SESAME SALMON

4 salmon steaks, 1 inch thick
4 eggs
Salt
Pepper
Monosodium glutamate, optional
Sesame seeds
1 small jar tiny sweet pickles and pickle liquid
Melted butter
Lemon slices

Beat eggs lightly; add salt, pepper, and monosodium glutamate (not necessary, but does make salmon moister). Dip salmon steak into egg mixture and press into sesame seeds until completely covered. Sprinkle steaks generously with liquid from pickles and arrange each on a sheet of foil. Fold loosely to cover. Broil 15 minutes on each side or until salmon tests flaky. Just before steaks are completely cooked, carefully fold foil back and let them brown. Serve on a warm platter. Garnish with melted butter, lemon slices, and whole sweet pickles. Serves four.

47

SALMON BUFFET

7 cups water
1 cup dry white wine
2 medium celery stalks, sliced
1 medium onion, sliced
1 tablespoon salt
½ teaspoon peppercorns
1 envelope chicken-flavor bouillon
1 6-pound whole salmon dressed, with head and tail on
3 eggs
3 medium tomatoes
3 lemons
Parsley sprigs for garnish
Confetti Sauce, Mustard Sauce, and Green Mayonnaise (recipes follow)

In 26-inch fish poacher, over high heat, heat first 7 ingredients to boiling (the poacher will require 2 heating units).

Rinse salmon under running cold water. Place salmon on poaching rack; lower rack with salmon into boiling liquid in fish poacher; over high heat, heat to boiling. Reduce heat to low; cover and simmer 30 minutes or until fish flakes easily when tested with fork. Remove rack from poacher. With two pancake turners, place salmon on large platter; cover and refrigerate until well chilled.

Meanwhile, prepare Confetti Sauce, Mustard Sauce, and Green Mayonnaise; cover and refrigerate. Hard-cook eggs; refrigerate.

(continued)

To serve:
Carefully cut skin around top half of salmon; remove and discard skin. Slice tomatoes, lemons, and hard-cooked eggs: arrange on platter with salmon. Garnish with parsley sprigs. Serve with all three sauces. Serves twelve.

Confetti sauce:
Drain and reserve ½ cup liquid from one 16-ounce jar pickled mixed vegetables; dice pickled mixed vegetables. In large bowl with fork, combine reserved liquid, ½ cup olive or salad oil, 4 teaspoons tarragon vinegar, and ½ teaspoon salt until well blended. Stir in diced vegetables; refrigerate until well chilled.

Mustard sauce:
In blender at medium speed, blend ½ cup mustard, ½ cup olive or salad oil, 2 tablespoons sugar, 3 tablespoons dry white wine, 1 tablespoon sour cream, and ¼ teaspoon salt until blended. Stir in ¼ teaspoon dill weed, and 1 teaspoon minced parsley; refrigerate until chilled.

Green Mayonnaise:
In blender at medium speed, blend 1 cup mayonnaise, 2 tablespoons chopped parsley, 2 teaspoons tarragon vinegar, ¼ teaspoon salt, and 1 sliced green onion until smooth.

SALMON AND PASTA

8 ounces pasta shells
½ pound salmon steak
½ cup dry white wine
½ cup water
6 sprigs parsley
1 bay leaf
1 clove garlic
1 teaspoon salt
3 carrots
1 cup boiling salted water
1 cup Italian olives, pitted and halves
2 tablespoons capers, rinsed
Dressing (recipe follows)

Cook pasta according to package directions. Drain and run under cold water. Cook salmon in the wine, ½ cup water, parsley, bay leaf, garlic and salt for 10 minutes. Remove skin and bones. Flake the steak and refrigerate. Cook carrots in the 1 cup boiling water for 10 minutes. Drain and slice into small pieces. Mix dressing ingredients and toss lightly with the pasta, salmon, carrots and olives. Chill slightly before serving.

Dressing:
½ cup olive oil
¼ cup lemon juice
1 tablespoon Dijon-style mustard
1 clove minced garlic
1 teaspoon crushed dried tarragon
½ teaspoon salt
¼ teaspoon freshly ground black pepper

SALMON SAUCE FOR PASTA

1 pound linguini
½ cup clam juice
½ cup white wine
6 tablespoons butter
3 cups cream
2 cups cook salmon, flaked
¼ cup fresh mint
Salt and pepper

Combine clam juice with wine and 3 tablespoons of butter. Bring to boil and reduce to 1/3 cup. Simmer cream until reduced by one-third. Combine with clam juice. Add salmon and mint. Salt and pepper to taste. Remove from heat and keep warm. Cook pasta in salted water, drain and toss with remaining butter. Toss pasta with sauce. Serve on heated plates and garnish with mint leaves. Serves four.

SALMON CHOPS

1½ cups cold cooked salmon
1 tablespoon lemon juice
2 tablespoons butter
1 cup milk
½ teaspoon paprika
3 tablespoons flour

Pick up the fish with a fork and free it from skin and bones, making it very fine. Sprinkle with lemon juice, paprika, and a dash of white pepper.

Make white sauce with butter, milk, and flour; salt and pepper to taste, and add a dash of minced parsley. As soon as done, stir into the minced fish. Mix thoroughly and spread in pan to cool. When thoroughly cold, shape into chops; crumb and egg, and fry in deep fat. Serves four.

SALMON POTATO CHEESE SOUP

1 pound salmon, cooked and broken into chunks
2 cups onion, sliced
1¼ cups celery, diced
¼ cup butter
4 medium potatoes, diced
1 cup chicken broth
3 cups milk
1 cup cream
2 cups sharp Cheddar cheese, grated
1 teaspoon thyme
1 tablespoon Worcestershire sauce
2 tablespoons fresh parsley, minced
Salt and pepper to taste

Saute onion and celery in butter until tender. Add potatoes and chicken broth; cook until potatoes are tender, about 20 minutes. Add milk, cream cheese, thyme, Worcestershire sauce and salmon. Season with salt and pepper. Cook, stirring until salmon is hot and cheese is melted. Garnish with minced parsley. Serves six.

SALMON RAMEKINS

¾ pound salmon, skinned and boned
2 tablespoons butter or margarine
1/3 cup sliced canned water chestnuts
1/3 cup chopped green onions
1 can (10½ ounces) white sauce
2 teaspoons Dijon mustard
1 tablespoon dry Sherry (optional)
⅛ teaspoon salt
⅛ teaspoon liquid hot pepper seasoning
1 ½ tablespoons grated parmesan cheese
1 ½ tablespoons fine dry bread crumbs
Paprika

Cut salmon into bite-sized pieces. Melt 1 tablespoon butter in a frying pan over medium heat; add salmon and cook, stirring often. Remove from heat, drain off all liquid, then stir in water chestnuts, onions, white sauce, mustard, Sherry (if used), salt, and hot pepper seasoning. Divide mixture evenly between two lightly buttered (about 1½ cup size) baking dishes. Combine cheese and crumbs; sprinkle evenly over tops and then dot with remaining butter. Dust each with paprika. Bake, uncovered, in a 425° oven for 15 minutes, or until bubbly. Serves two.

BOILED SALMON

1 whole fresh salmon (about 8 pounds)
2 tablespoons vinegar
1 large onion, sliced
4 celery stalks with leaves
Salt, to season
Peppercorns, to season
½ pound melted butter

Leave head on cleaned salmon. Fill fish pan with enough water to cover salmon. Add vinegar, onion, celery, salt and peppercorns. Bring water to boil; add fish. Cover and poach fish, over medium-low flame, not allowing water to boil, for 12 minutes per pound or until tender. Drain and serve hot with melted butter. In Iceland, boiled potatoes usually are served with the salmon. Serves ten.

BOILED SALMON
WITH HORSERADISH

2 fresh salmon fillets (about 3 pounds)
1 quart water
¼ cup butter, melted
1 tablespoon parsley, chopped
½ pound horseradish root, grated
Salt and pepper
1 pint cream

Salt fresh fillets and let stand several hours. Place in fish kettle with boiling salt water for ½ hour or until well-cooked. Lift out carefully and place on a hot platter and pour over ½ cupful of melted butter; sprinkle well with 1 tablespoon of parsley. Serve with the following sauce:

Peel ½ pound of horseradish root, grate and mix well with 1 pint of cream beaten stiff. Serves six.

SALMON WELLINGTON

1½ pound salmon fillets
1 package (10 ounces) frozen pastry shells
Mushroom filling (recipe follows) Lemon or
Sherry Sauce (recipe follows)
Poaching liquid:
2 cups water
1 cup dry wine
1 small carrot, sliced
1 onion, sliced
1 bay leaf
10 whole black peppers
4 whole allspice
½ teaspoon each salt and thyme leaves
3 sprigs parsley

In a wide frying pan, combine water, wine, carrot, onion, bay leaf, peppers, allspice, salt and thyme leaves, and 3 sprigs parsley. Cover and simmer 15 minutes.

Cut salmon into 6 pieces, each about 3 inches square; place in poaching liquid with skin-side down. Cover and gently simmer just until salmon is almost light pink throughout, about 7 to 10 minutes. With a spatula, lift salmon (discard skin) from pan. Cool, then cover and chill. Reserve poaching liquid.

Mushroom filling:
1 tablespoon butter or margarine
½ pound mushrooms, sliced
2 green onions, sliced

Melt butter or margarine in a frying pan over medium heat. Add mushrooms and onions. Cook, stirring, about 5 to 10 minutes or until liquid evaporates. Cool, cover, and chill.

(continued)

55

Pastry:
Thaw 1 package (10 ounces) frozen pastry shells. For each piece of salmon, roll out a thawed patty shell on a floured board to make an 8-inch circle. Spoon 1 tablespoon mushroom filling in center and set a piece of salmon on top. Place Wellingtons with folded side down on an ungreased rimmed baking sheet. Cover and chill.

Before serving, place uncovered on the lowest rack of a 425° oven. Bake for 10 minutes. Move pan to highest rack and bake for 8 to 10 minutes more, or until pastry is golden brown. Serve at once with Lemon or Sherry sauce. Serves six.

Lemon or Sherry Sauce:
Poaching liquid
1 tablespoon cornstarch
3 egg yolks
3 tablespoons lemon juice or dry sherry

Strain reserved poaching liquid, discarding vegetables. Boil liquid, uncovered, over high heat until reduced to 1½ cups (or add water to make 1½ cups). Stir together 1 tablespoon each cornstarch and water; add to poaching liquid and cook, stirring, until sauce boils and thickens.

Beat 3 egg yolks with 2 to 3 tablespoons lemon juice or dry Sherry. Stir some of the hot sauce into the yolk mixture, then return all to pan. Cook, stirring, over very low heat just until thickened. Cover and chill if made ahead. To reheat, place in the top of a double boiler over hot water; stir often and remove when hot.

SALMON FLORENTINE

4 tablespoons butter or margarine
1 large onion, chopped
1½ to 2 pounds fresh spinach, shredded
1½ cups water
1 tablespoon lemon juice
Salt and pepper
2 pounds salmon fillets
2 tablespoons all-purpose flour
1 teaspoon Dijon mustard
2 tablespoons grated Parmesan cheese

Melt 2 tablespoons of the butter in a large frying pan over medium heat; and saute onions. Add spinach to pan, cover, and cook just until wilted. Turn into a shallow 2-quart baking dish.

Pour water into pan, add lemon juice, dash salt and pepper, and salmon. Cover and simmer until fish flakes when probed, about 10 minutes. Lift out fish and arrange on spinach. Reserve 1 cup poaching liquid.

Melt remaining 2 tablespoons butter in pan; stir in flour and cook until bubbly. Add the reserved poaching liquid and cook, stirring, until thickened. Season with salt, pepper, mustard, and cheese. Pour over fish. Bake, uncovered, in a 350° oven 20 minutes or until hot through. Serves four.

SALMON STEAKS
WITH JADE SAUCE

½ cup butter
2 tablespoons each parsley and green onions, minced
2 tablespoons lemon juice
4 salmon steaks, ¾-inch thick
Lemon wedges

   Wipe salmon steaks with paper towel before brushing with melted butter. Broil 4 inches from heat for 10 minutes; turn salmon and brush with butter. Broil 8 minutes longer or until salmon flakes easily. While salmon is broiling, melt remaining butter, stir in parsley, onion and lemon juice; keep warm. Place salmon on platter and spoon on sauce. Arrange lemon wedges. Serves four.

SALMON SCALLOPS WITH PEAS

1 pound salmon fillets
3 tablespoons unsalted butter
Salt and pepper to taste
½ pound each snow peas and fresh baby peas
1 teaspoon sugar
1 sprig tarragon

   Melt butter in a large skillet. Cut salmon fillets into scallop size. Saute salmon over high heat. Turn salmon once; place on a heated platter. In same skillet, add ½ cup of water and bring to a boil. Add peas, sugar and tarragon. Cook over high heat 2-3 minutes until peas are tender. Spoon peas over salmon. Serves three.

SALMON WITH MUSTARD-CAPER SAUCE

4 salmon steaks, 1 inch thick
1/3 cup dry white wine
¼ cup whipping cream
1 ½ teaspoons Dijon mustard
2 egg yolks
1 tablespoon capers, drained
Salt and white pepper

Pat fish dry. Arrange in a shallow 2-quart glass baking dish with meaty portions toward edges of dish; add wine. Cover dish with heavy plastic wrap and cook in microwave oven on high (100%) for 5 minutes; let stand, covered, for 5 minutes. Turn fish over, cover and cook in microwave on high for 2-4 minutes or until fish flakes with fork in thickest portion. Transfer fish to a platter; cover and chill. Pour fish liquid and cream into a small pan; boil until reduced to ½ cup liquid. Blend mustard and yolks; stir in part of the hot liquid; stir back into liquid in pan. Cook over low heat, stirring, 1 to 2 minutes or until sauce thickens slightly. Stir in capers and salt and pepper to taste. Cover and chill. Spoon part of the sauce over fish; serve with remaining sauce. Serves four.

SALMON AND MUSHROOMS

4 salmon steaks, ¾-inch thick
½ teaspoon salt
¼ cup butter
1 small onion, chopped
1 stalk celery, chopped
3 cups bread, cubed
3 cups fresh mushrooms, sliced
2 tablespoons parsley, chopped
1 tablespoon lemon juice
¼ cup cream

In a greased low baking pan, arrange salmon steaks and season with ¼ teaspoon salt. In a large skillet, saute onion and celery in butter until tender. Addbread, mushrooms, parsley, ¼ teaspoon salt, and lemon juice; mix well. Spoon stuffing on top of salmon steaks. Drizzle cream over top. Bake in preheated oven at 350° for 25-30 minutes. Serves four.

BAKED SALMON
WITH CUCUMBER SAUCE

2 to 3 pounds salmon
Butter
Salt and pepper
1 cup sour cream or yogurt
2 teaspoons chopped parsley
½ teaspoon chopped chives
½ medium cucumber, peeled and finely chopped
or shredded
2 teaspoons lemon juice

Heat oven to 350°. Place salmon in greased shallow baking pan; brush with butter and season with salt and pepper. Bake uncovered for 30-50 minutes or until fish flakes easily. Section salmon; remove large bones and place on heat-proof platter. In a small bowl, combine remaining ingredients; spoon over salmon. Return to oven for 5 minutes to heat sauce. Serves four.

BAKED SALMON
WITH SOUR CREAM STUFFING

4-6 pounds dressed salmon
1½ teaspoon salt
Sour Cream Stuffing (recipe follows)
2 tablespoons oil

Thaw frozen salmon. Clean, wash and dry fish; sprinkle inside and out with salt. Stuff fish loosely with Sour Cream Stuffing. Close opening with small skewers or toothpicks. Place fish in a well greased baking pan; brush with fat. Bake in 350° oven for 1 hour or until fish flakes easily with a fork. Baste occasionally with fat. Remove skewers. Serves six to eight.

Sour Cream Stuffing:
¾ cup chopped celery
½ cup chopped onion
¼ cup melted fat or oil
1 quart dry bread crumbs
1 teaspoon salt
½ cup sour cream
¼ cup diced peeled lemon
2 tablespoons grated lemon rind
1 teaspoon paprika

Cook celery and onion in oil until tender. Combine all ingredients and mix thoroughly. Makes 1 quart stuffing.

BAKED STUFFED SALMON

1 (10- to 12-pound) salmon fillet
1 tablespoon salt
3 tablespoons lemon juice
1 cup chopped celery
1 cup chopped celery leaves
2 small onions, finely chopped
¼ cup butter or margarine
¼ pound mushrooms, sliced
1 loaf whole-wheat bread, crumbed
2 teaspoons poultry seasoning
1 teaspoon salt
⅛ teaspoon pepper
1 bottle (8 ounces) stuffed olives, chopped

Rub salmon well inside and out with salt; sprinkle with lemon juice. Saute celery, leaves, and onions in butter until onion is transparent. Add mushrooms; cook 5 minutes longer. Add crumbs, seasonings and olives. Place stuffing in one side of salmon; sew fish together. Lay fish on greased baking sheet. Bake at 425°, allowing 10 minutes per pound. Baste frequently. The fish should be tender but not dry. Serves eight.

BAKED SALMON
WITH CREAM AND CUCUMBER

3-pound salmon, cleaned
1 tablespoon butter
1 medium-sized cucumber, peeled and cubed
Salt and pepper
½ pint (1 cup) cream
Juice of 1 lemon
2 sprigs of parsley

Put the parsley in the cleaned gullet of the fish and rub the butter over the outside. Put the whole fish into a fireproof baking dish, season well and pour the cream around. Cover with foil and bake in a moderate oven at 350° for 30 minutes. Remove from the oven and add the peeled and cubed cucumber and the lemon juice. Baste well and put back in the oven, uncovered, for a further 15 minutes. Skin the fish before serving and pour over the sauce. It is excellent hot, but can also be served cold. Serves four.

BAKED STUFFED SALMON

3-pound salmon
2 tablespoons onion, chopped
2 tablespoons butter or margarine
1½ cups bread, diced
½ cup cottage cheese
1 teaspoon fresh dill, chopped
1 tablespoon dill pickle, finely chopped
½ teaspoon salt
Dash of pepper
2 teaspoons lemon juice
Melted butter or margarine

Saute onion in butter or margarine; add bread; mix well. Add cottage cheese, dill, dill pickle, salt, pepper, and lemon juice; mix thoroughly. Wash and dry fish. Sprinkle inside fish with salt; fill with stuffing; close with wooden picks or skewers. Place fish in lightly greased baking pan. Brush lightly with melted butter or margarine. Bake in hot oven (400°) for 30 minutes. Serves four.

BAKED SALMON STEAKS
WITH ONION, LEMON
AND PARSLEY

2 cups minced onion
4 tablespoons butter or margarine
¼ cup minced parsley
2 tablespoons lemon juice (or to taste)
4 salmon steaks, 1½ inches thick
½ teaspoon salt
⅛ teaspoon pepper

Saute the onion in the butter in a medium-sized skillet over moderate heat about 5 minutes or until golden and limp; mix in parsley and lemon juice. Sprinkle the salmon steaks well on both sides with salt and pepper, then place in a shallow roasting pan just large enough to accommodate the steaks. Spread onion mixture on top of each steak, dividing total amount evenly. Cover pan snugly with foil. Bake in a moderate oven (350°) for 10 minutes, then uncover and bake 15 to 20 minutes longer or just until fish will flake at the touch of a fork. Serves four.

SIMPLE BAKED SALMON

3 pounds salmon
Salt and pepper
1 tablespoon lemon juice
2 cups sour cream
Any or all of the following:
1 tablespoon chopped dill
1 tablespoon chopped chives
2 tablespoons chopped parsley

Salt and pepper a piece of salmon or salmon steaks lightly and place in a greased baking dish. Mix together remaining ingredients and spread over salmon. Bake in 375° oven for 30 minutes or until salmon flakes to fork test. Serves six.

BAKED SALMON

4 salmon steaks, 1 inch thick
1 onion, chopped
1 cup mushrooms, sliced
1 tablespoon parsley
1 tomato, cubed
1 clove garlic, chopped

Season with salt and pepper and add a few drops of lemon juice. Cook in moderately hot oven (350°) for 20 to 25 minutes, using well-buttered baking dish. Add chopped onions, fresh mushrooms, parsley, tomatoes and just a suggestion of chopped garlic. Serves four.

BAKED SALMON

1 whole salmon, 8-10 pounds
¼ cup melted butter
1 lemon, ¼ inch slices
1 onion, ½-inch slices
Salt and pepper

Basting sauce:
½ cup water
½ cup white wine
2 tablespoons butter

Rub salmon cavity with lemon juice. Sprinkle with salt and pepper. Let stand at room temperature 30 minutes. Line baking pan with buttered foil. Brush salmon with melted butter on both sides and place on foil. Stuff cavity with lemon and onion slices. Bake 35-45 minutes at 425°. Make basting sauce by bringing ingredients to boil and simmering 5 minutes. Baste salmon 2-8 times during cooking. Serves six.

BAKED SALMON
WITH MOUSSE TOPPING

½ pound lingcod or sole fillets, skinned
1 egg
½ cup whipping cream
4 salmon steaks, 1 inch thick
1 cup dry white wine
½ teaspoon thyme leaves
1 green onion, chopped
4 tablespoons butter or margarine
Salt and pepper
Watercress sprigs

Puree fish fillets. Add the egg and ¼ cup of the cream; mix well to blend thoroughly. Arrange salmon steaks side by side in a 9-inch by 13-inch baking dish. Evenly spread the fish mixture over each.

Just before baking, pour wine around steaks. Bake, uncovered, in a 450° oven for 15 minutes or until mousse is delicately browned and salmon flakes when prodded with a fork in the thickest portion.

With a spatula, carefully transfer steaks to warm dinner plates; keep warm. Pour cooking liquid through a wire strainer into a 10- to 12-inch frying pan. Add cream, thyme, and green onion and boil, stirring rapidly, until reduced to ½ cup. Remove the pan from heat or turn heat to low.

With wire whip or spoon, stir in the butter, a lump at a time, blending constantly to incorporate quickly the melting butter, which thickens the sauce. Season to taste with salt and pepper.

Spoon sauce around salmon steaks. Garnish each serving with a cluster of watercress. Serves four.

BAKED SALMON
WITH VEGETABLE STUFFING

8- to 10-pound salmon
Salt and pepper to taste
½ cup butter, melted
¼ cup lemon juice
Salad oil
Stuffing (recipe follows)

Heat oven to 350°. Wash fish and pat dry. Rub cavity with salt and pepper. Stuff with stuffing. Close with skewers and lace with string. Brush salmon with salad oil. Cook in shallow roasting pan for about 1½ hours or until fish flakes easily with fork. Baste occasionally with mixture of butter and lemon juice during baking. This can also be done over a barbecue if you have a fish wire basket so it can be turned often.

Stuffing:
1 cup onions, chopped
¼ cup butter
2 cups dry bread cubes
1 cup shredded carrots
1 cup sliced mushrooms
½ cup snipped parsley
1½ tablespoons lemon juice
1 egg
1 clove garlic, minced
2 teaspoons salt
¼ teaspoon marjoram leaves
¼ teaspoon pepper

Cook onion in butter until tender. Lightly mix in remaining ingredients.

BAKED SALMON

1 salmon, 6-8 pounds, cleaned
1 cup carrots, sliced thin
1 cup onions, sliced thin
¼ cup shallots, sliced thin
1 cup celery, sliced thin
½ teaspoon thyme
Salt
8 peppercorns, crushed
1 clove garlic, crushed
1 bay leaf
2 cups dry white wine

Line a baking sheet with heavy foil. Place salmon in the center of the foil and add carrots, onions, shallots, celery, thyme, salt, peppercorns, garlic, bay leaf and wine. Fold foil and seal. Place in preheated oven at 400° and bake for 50 minutes. Remove and place on platter. Serves eight.

SALMON BAKED IN A BLANKET

4- to 5-pound salmon
Lemon juice
3 tablespoon butter
3 cups flour
Salt and pepper
Lemon wedges

Season fish inside and out with salt and pepper. Sprinkle with lemon juice and dot with butter. Make a thick paste of flour and water. Cover entire fish with paste; place on greased baking sheet. Bake in preheated very hot oven (450°) for 25 to 30 minutes. Remove from oven. Crack crust and remove fish carefully. Discard crust. Serve fish with lemon. Serves six.

BAKED SALMON
WITH FRUITS AND HERBS

4 salmon steaks, 1 inch thick
3 tablespoons lemon juice
1 lemon cut in 8 slices
1 orange cut in 8 slices
2 limes cut in 8 slices
Salt and pepper
16 basil leaves cut in strips
8 mint leaves, chopped
Parchment paper

Cut 4 squares of parchment. On 1 square arrange a line of alternating citrus slices using 2 slices of each type. Place salmon to cover about half of the slices, sprinkle with lemon juice and season with salt and pepper. Sprinkle each salmon with mint and basil. Seal the parchment squares and bake on a baking sheet 10 minutes at 375°. Serves four.

BAKED SALMON

1 whole fish, cleaned
Thyme
Butter
Several strips of bacon
Aluminum foil

Put salmon on heavy foil large enough to fold over and seal. Dot with butter, sprinkle with thyme and put several strips of bacon on top. Seal foil. Bake at 350° for 1 hour, or 15 minutes per inch of thickness measured at its thickest part. Holds well in warm oven. Discard bacon before serving.

SALMON BAKED IN FOIL

1 whole salmon (6 to 8 pounds), preferably with head on, cleaned
1 cup thinly sliced carrots
1 cup thinly sliced onions
1 cup thinly sliced celery
¼ cup thinly sliced shallots
1 tablespoon salt, or to taste
8 peppercorns, crushed
1 clove garlic, unpeeled, crushed
1 bay leaf
½ teaspoon thyme
2 cups dry white wine
White-Wine Sauce (recipe follows)

On baking sheet large enough to accommodate fish, lay out a double length heavy duty foil with foil extending at both ends. Place salmon in center of foil; turn up sides. Add carrots, onions, celery, shallots, salt,peppercorns, garlic, bay leaf, thyme and wine. Bring up ends of foil; fold together to seal. Tightly crimp sides of foil to seal completely. Bake in pre-heated 400° oven 50 minutes. Loosen foil; test fish for doneness (back center fin should be easy to remove when pulled with fingers). If necessary, continue cooking 10 minutes or until done. Serve hot with White-Wine Sauce. Serves 12.

White Wine Sauce:
2 cups strained salmon cooking broth
Vegetables and seasonings from the baked salmon and strained broth
1 cup heavy cream
2 tablespoons butter or margarine, softened
2 tablespoons flour
¼ cup cold butter or margarine, cut in small pieces
1 tablespoon lemon juice
½ teaspoon salt
Cayenne pepper to taste

(continued)

73

In saucepan, bring to boil strained broth, vegetables and seasonings from fish. Reduce heat, simmer 15 minutes or until liquid is reduced to 1½ cups. Strain broth; return to saucepan. Add cream. Blend softened butter and flour until a smooth paste. Bring sauce to simmer and, stirring constantly, gradually add butter-flour mixture until thick and smooth. Gradually stir in pieces of cold butter, then lemon juice, salt and cayenne. Remove from heat. Makes 3 cups.

SALMON IN PARCHMENT

4 salmon steaks, 1 inch thick
Salt
Garlic powder
1 large onion, sliced
1 bay leaf
1/3 cup melted butter or margarine
Lemon juice
Parchment

Wipe steaks with a damp cloth. Sprinkle on both sides with salt and garlic powder. Use a piece of parchment, cutting a piece 16 inches by 20 inches. Grease paper thoroughly with pastry brush and place on a shallow roasting pan. Put steaks on paper and top with onion, bay leaf, melted butter and lemon juice. Wrap paper tightly around steaks, folding in ends. Pinch ends together. Bake in preheated hot oven (425°) for 25 minutes. Unwrap, discard bay leaf and serve immediately. Serves four.

SALMON IN PAPILLOTE

12 thin slices of salmon (2 ounces each)
2-3 tomatoes, peeled, seeded and cubed (2 cups)
6 large mushrooms, sliced (1½ cups)
6 sprigs fresh thyme
6 sprigs fresh tarragon
1½ cups loosely packed parsley leaves
Salt and freshly ground black pepper
4 tablespoons butter (optional)
6 (18-inch by 12-inch) pieces of lightly oiled waxed paper

Cut the slices of salmon on a bias about ¼ inch thick. Arrange tomatoes and mushrooms on one side of paper piece and place 2 salmon slices on top. Sprinkle with salt, pepper and some parsley leaves. Top with a sprig of thyme and tarragon. Fold the paper back on the fish. Start folding the edge of the papillote to encase the fish. Keep folding all around, making sure each of the pleats is well secured. As you keep folding the edges, the papillote will take on an oval shape. Come to the end and leave a small opening. Insert a straw in the opening and blow into the straw to inflate the papillote. Remove straw and twist the opening to prevent air from escaping.

Place on a cookie sheet in a 425° oven for 10 minutes. The papillote should brown slightly and stay inflated. Lift one end and slide a large spatula underneath. Place on a serving plate and using a knife or scissors, cut a cross in the paper in front of the guest. Fold the 4 corners open to expose the fish. Top with 2 teaspoons butter for each serving, if desired. Serves six.

S·M·O·K·E·D S·A·L·M·O·N

SMOKED SALMON SOUP

2 tablespoons butter
2 medium onions, chopped
1 green pepper, chopped
1 large garlic clove, minced
2 cans stewed tomatoes
12 ounces smoked salmon, chopped
2 tablespoons minced parsley
1 bay leaf
½ teaspoon thyme leaves
1 tablespoon Worcestershire
¼ teaspoon liquid hot pepper
2 tablespoons lemon juice
½ cup red wine
½ cup chicken broth

Melt butter in a large pan. Add onions, green pepper and garlic. Cook until tender. Add tomatoes, wine and broth. Add chopped salmon to soup with parsley, bay leaf, thyme, Worcestershire and hot pepper seasoning. Cover and simmer 15 minutes. Stir in lemon juice and salt and pepper. Serves four.

SMOKED SALMON CORNETS

2 pounds smoked salmon, thinly sliced
1½ cups heavy cream
Beluga caviar (about 12 tablespoons)
Fresh chives

Slice salmon into 24 three-inch squares. Roll salmon squares into a hollow cone. Whip cream until very thick and stuff each cone with about 2 tablespoons whipped cream. Top cornets with caviar and garnish with fresh chives. Serves six.

SMOKED SALMON CHOWDER

3 tablespoons butter
1 small onion, minced
1 large celery stalk, minced
1 large potato, cut into 1-inch cubes
2 tablespoons flour
1 cup fish stock, clam broth, chicken stock or water
1 cup water
3 fresh parsley sprigs
1 bay leaf
½ teaspoon thyme, crumbled
8 ounces boned smoked salmon, cut into 1-inch cubes
1 cup milk
½ cup whipping cream
Freshly ground pepper
Snipped fresh chives
Prepared white horseradish

Melt butter. Add onion and celery. Cook ten minutes. Add potato cubes and cook about three minutes. Sprinkle mixture with flour and stir. Blend in broth, water, and spices. Bring to a boil and simmer until potato is tender. Add salmon, milk and cream to the chowder until hot. Discard bay leaf and parsley sprigs. Sprinkle with chives, black pepper and horseradish to taste. Serves six.

SMOKED SALMON PIZZA

3-6 ounces smoked salmon, sliced
4 ounces cream cheese at room temperature
1 teaspoon dill weed
1 piece knacker brod (large round rye cracker)
½ cup sliced green onion
1 hard-cooked egg, sliced

Blend cream cheese and dill weed. Spread on one piece knacker brod. Top with sliced salmon and sprinkle with green onion. Broil 4 to 6 inches from heat for about 1 minute or until hot. Garnish with sliced egg and serve at once. Serves two.

SMOKED SALMON
AND AVOCADO SALAD

1 large avocado
3 ounces smoked salmon
8 ounces unflavored yogurt
1 lemon

Halve the avocado and remove seed. Pile salmon into each avocado half; spoon yogurt over the top; squeeze on lemon juice. Serves two.

SMOKED SALMON
WITH NOODLES AND CHEESE

1 stick butter
4 tablespoons flour
2 ½ cups milk
Pinch of nutmeg
2 ounces cognac
12 ounces of very thin noodles, cooked and drained
6 ounces smoked salmon, thinly sliced and cut into narrow strips
2/3 cup grated Gruyere cheese
2/3 cup grated Parmesan cheese

Cook over low heat 4 tablespoons butter and flour (stirring constantly) until you have a smooth paste. Add milk slowly and stir until you have a smooth sauce. Add nutmeg, cognac, salt and pepper. Set aside. Mix the cooked pasta with the rest of butter. Place 1/3 of pasta in buttered baking dish. Layer ½ of salmon strips with 1/3 of cheeses. Pour a thin layer of sauce over cheese. Arrange another layer of pasta, rest of salmon, 1/3 cheese and another thin layer of sauce. Cover with rest of pasta and sauce. Sprinkle the rest of cheese on top. Bake in 350° oven for 20 minutes or until top is golden. Serves six.

SMOKED SALMON SALAD
AND EGG

2 hard-cooked eggs, chilled
3 ounces watercress
6 ounces lightly smoked salmon
¼ cup lemon juice
1/3 cup olive oil
¼ teaspoon dill weed
¼ teaspoon dry mustard
¼ teaspoon sugar
Dash pepper
1 tablespoon drained capers

Wash watercress and arrange on four salad plates. Divide salmon into four equal portions; roll up slices and arrange on watercress. Peel eggs and cut in half lengthwise. Place half an egg on each plate next to the salmon roll. Mix the rest of ingredients until well-blended. Pour over salad. Serves four.

SMOKED SALMON AND DILL-STUFFED POTATOES

4 baking potatoes, scrubbed and dry
4 teaspoons shortening
3 tablespoon butter
¼ cup heavy cream
½ cup boned smoked salmon, chopped
2 hardboiled eggs, chopped
1/3 cup snipped fresh dill or 1 tablespoon dried
¼ cup Parmesan oheese

Rub potatoes all over with shortening to keep skins soft. Bake at 425° degrees for 1 hour. Cut baked potato lengthwise and scoop out pulp. Mash pulp; add butter and cream and beat until fluffy. Add the remaining ingredients and blend. Mound the filling into the potato shells. Bake potatoes on a baking sheet at 425° for 15 minutes. Serves four.

SMOKED SALMON AND SCOTCH WHISKY

12 ounces rigatoni pasta
3 tablespoons butter
1 large shallot, chopped
2 tablespoons lemon juice
3 ounces smoked salmon, finely chopped
1 cup heavy cream
4 ounces Scotch whisky
Salt and white pepper to taste

Cook pasta and drain. Melt butter in a large skillet. Add shallots and cook for one minute. Add salmon and cook for two minutes. Add lemon juice and mix well. Stir in Scotch and cream and cook mixture until alcohol evaporates. Add salt and white pepper to taste Add well-drained pasta to salmon mixture. Stir gently until pasta is well-coated. Serves six.

SMOKED SALMON
AND RICE SALAD

8 ounces smoked salmon
3 cups cooked long-grained rice
1 cup celery, sliced
1 package (10 ounces) frozen peas (thawed)
½ cup green onions, sliced (including part of green tops)
¼ cup pimento, diced
3 hard cooked eggs chopped (save a few slices for garnish)
½ cup mayonnaise
½ cup plain yogurt or sour cream
1 teaspoon curry powder
2 tablespoons parsley, finely chopped
½ teaspoon salt
½ teaspoon dry basil
1 tablespoon lemon juice
Dash cayenne

Steam salmon for about 15 minutes. Remove and cool. Flake fish and remove skin and bone. Spread rice in a shallow bowl. Over rice arrange salmon, celery, peas, onions, pimento and egg. Chill. Mix remaining ingredients. When ready to serve, mix dressing with salad and top with egg slices. Serves four to six.

SMOKED SALMON CASSEROLE

½ pound smoked salmon
1 cup sliced green onions
2 eggs, hard cooked
4 servings instant mashed potatoes
1½ cups milk
½ teaspoon thyme leaves
½ teaspoon parsley flakes
¼ teaspoon ground nutmeg
¼ teaspoon salt
¼ teaspoon pepper
¼ cup shredded Parmesan cheese
2 tablespoons butter
2 tablespoons all-purpose flour

Flake salmon and remove skin and bone. Distribute in quart casserole. Sprinkle onions over fish. Reserve 1/3 cup onions for garnish. Arrange egg slices on top. Prepare instant potatoes according to package instructions. Cover and set aside. Melt butter over medium heat. Add flour and cook until bubbly. Gradually stir in milk until sauce boils and thickens. Add seasonings and spoon sauce over ingredients in the casserole. Spoon the potatoes around edge of casserole. Sprinkle potatoes with cheese. Bake uncovered in a 400° oven until potatoes are browned. Garnish with reserved green onion. Serves four.

SMOKED SALMON AND DILL CHEESECAKE

½ cup fine bread crumbs
1 large onion, chopped
3 tablespoons butter
3 packages cream cheese (8 ounces each) at room temperature
8 ounces smoked salmon
4 eggs
1 tablespoon lemon juice
1 tablespoon fresh dill, minced
Garnish with dill sprigs and strips of smoked salmon

Grease an 8-inch springform pan. Sprinkle bread crumbs in pan to coat bottom and sides halfway up; refrigerate. Cook onion in a small skillet with butter over medium heat, about 5 minutes. Process cream cheese until smooth. Add salmon, cooked onion, eggs, lemon juice and dill. Process until smooth.

Pour mixture into the springform pan. Place in large deeper baking pan. Place in the center of a 325° preheated oven. Pour hot water into the larger pan until halfway up the sides of the springform pan. Bake 1 hour. Cool in oven 1 hour with door slightly ajar. Remove pan from water and place on cooling rack; refrigerate. Remove sides of pan and garnish accordingly. Best served at room temperature. Serves eight.

SMOKED SALMON
WITH CELERY ROOT

1 pound celery root, peeled and sliced ⅛ inch
1 small onion, chopped
12 ounces smoked salmon
2 tablespoons butter
2 tablespoons flour
¼ teaspoon sugar
½ teaspoon salt
Dash of pepper
¼ cup dry white wine
1 bay leaf
1½ cup milk
1 teaspoon parsley, chopped
1 tablespoon lemon juice
Lemon wedges

Place sliced celery root and chopped onion into a 10-inch frying pan. Add wine, bay leaf, salt and pepper. Remove skin and bone from salmon and set fish in center of pan. Cover pan and simmer until celery root is tender, about 20 minutes. Melt butter in a saucepan over medium heat. Stir in flour and cook until bubbly. Gradually add milk. Stir until sauce thickens. Stir in remaining ingredients. Pour sauce over fish in pan. Cover and leave over low heat for 5 minutes. Sprinkle with more parsley and serve with lemon wedges. Serves six.

SMOKED SALMON CHEESECAKE

½ cup onion, chopped
5 tablespoons grated Parmesan cheese
3 tablespoons fine bread crumbs
½ cup green pepper, chopped
3 tablespoons butter
3 ½ packages cream cheese (8 ounces each) at room temperature
4 eggs
½ cup heavy cream
5 ounces salmon, chopped
½ cup grated Gruyere cheese
Pepper

Butter an 8-inch springform pan. Sprinkle bottom and sides of prepared pan with bread crumbs and 2 tablespoons of Parmesan cheese until coated. Saute onion and green pepper in butter until tender. Beat cream cheese, eggs and cream together in a large bowl until smooth. Fold in salmon, the remaining Parmesan cheese, Gruyere cheese and the sauteed onion and green pepper; pepper to taste. Pour mixture into prepared pan. Set pan in slightly larger pan and pour hot water into larger pan to a depth of 2 inches. Place in the center of a preheated oven at 300° for 1 hour and 40 minutes. Turn heat off. Let cake sit in the oven 1 hour longer with oven door ajar. Lift cake out of water bath and cool on rack at room temperature; refrigerate. Remove from refrigerator 1 hour before serving. Loosen cake sides around the edge with a small knife. Add garnish of salmon slices and dill sprigs. Serves eight.

MOUSSELINE
OF SMOKED SALMON

16 ounces smoked boned salmon, diced
¾ cup sour cream
1 stick unsalted butter, softened
3 ounces black caviar
8 ounces smoked boned salmon, thinly sliced

Blend diced salmon and sour cream until smooth. Blend in butter and force it through a sieve. Put 3 ounces of the mousseline into bowl and gently fold in caviar; set aside. Line a loaf pan with parchment or waxed paper. Butter the paper and line with sliced salmon, slightly overlapping the slices and reserve some for the top. Fill the pan with half of the mousseline. Make a ½-inch deep cavity down the length of the mousseline. Fill the cavity with the caviar mixture. Cover with the remaining mousseline and top with remaining sliced salmon. Refrigerate overnight. Unmold and remove parchment paper. Slice with a warm knife. Serves six.

SMOKED SALMON DIP

4 ounces boned smoked salmon
¼ medium onion
½ teaspoon lemon juice
¼ teaspoon pepper
1 8-ounce package cream cheese, at room temperature
½ cup milk
1 tablespoon red salmon caviar
1 teaspoon scallion greens, thin sliced

Puree salmon, onion, lemon juice and pepper until smooth. Cut up cream cheese and add to salmon; pour in milk and process until well-blended. Stir in 2 teaspoons of the caviar and scrape dip into an attractive bowl. Cover and refrigerate 2 hours or up to 2 days. Garnish top with remaining caviar and scallion greens. Makes 2 cups.

C·A·N·N·E·D S·A·L·M·O·N

NORWEGIAN SALMON

1 can lobster, diced
1 jar caviar
½ teaspoon tarragon
1 tablespoon mustard
1 cup mayonnaise
Salt and pepper
3 small cucumbers, peeled
3 slices smoked salmon
6 very small tomatoes, peeled and hollowed out
½ small head iceberg lettuce, shredded
1 can (15½ ounces) salmon, flaked
1 lemon, sliced

Combine diced lobster with caviar, tarragon and mustard, season to taste and chill. Cut cucumbers in half the long way and scoop out seeds, making 6 little "boats." Mince or grind smoked salmon, put into boats and grind pepper over top. Put lobster sauce into tomatoes and arrange around a large serving platter covered with shredded lettuce. Set the cucumber boats between the tomatoes and center the platter with the flaked salmon. Garnish with lemon slices and serve. Serves six.

SALMON SUPPER

1 package (8 ounces) egg noodles
1 can (7 ¾ ounces) salmon, drained, reserving liquid
1 can (10 ¾ ounces) cream of celery soup
1 can (4 ounces) mushrooms, drained
½ cup mayonnaise
½ cup sliced ripe olives
1 tablespoon green onion, minced
1 can (2.8 ounces) french fried onions or crushed potato chips

Prepare egg noodles. In a bowl, break apart salmon; remove any bones and skin. Add salmon liquid, soup, mushrooms, mayonnaise, ripe olives and minced green onions. Mix together thoroughly and combine with drained noodles. Pour into buttered 2-quart casserole dish. Top with French fried onions; bake 350° for 30 minutes or until thoroughly heated. Makes 6 cups.

PASTA AND SALMON MEDLEY

¼ cup salad oil
1 small garlic clove, sliced
1 medium bunch broccoli, cut into 2-inch by ¼-inch pieces
¼ pound medium mushrooms, quartered
2 medium carrots, sliced
2 large green onions, cut into 1-inch pieces
Salt
1 12-ounce package fettuccine noodles
2 tablespoons butter or margarine
2 tablespoons all-purpose flour
2 ½ cups milk
1 chicken-flavor bouillon cube
¼ cup grated Parmesan cheese
1 7 ¾-ounce can salmon, drained and flaked

In 12-inch skillet over medium-high heat, cook garlic in oil until lightly browned; discard garlic. To hot oil add broccoli, mushrooms, carrots, green onions, and teaspoon salt; cook until vegetables are tender-crisp, about 5 minutes, stirring frequently.

Meanwhile, in 6-quart saucepot, prepare fettuccine noodles as label directs; drain. Return fettuccine to saucepot; keep warm.

In 2-quart saucepot over medium heat, melt butter or margarine. Stir in flour and ¼ teaspoon salt until blended. Gradually stir in milk and bouillon and cook, stirring constantly, until sauce is slightly thickened and smooth. Remove saucepot from heat; stir in cheese until melted.

To saucepot, add salmon, cheese sauce, and vegetables; over medium-low heat, heat through, gently tossing to mix well. Serves six.

SALMON AND NOODLES

Chicken-flavor Noodle Mix
Boiling water
1 package (10 ounces) frozen green peas, thawed
1 can (7 ¾ ounces) salmon, flaked
2 tablespoons green onions, sliced
1/3 cup mayonnaise or salad dressing
1/3 cup sour cream
1 tablespoon lemon juice
1 teaspoon Worcestershire sauce
Lemon wedges and parsley for garnish (optional)

Follow how-to-use procedure for Noodle Mix but omit the butter or margarine. In small bowl, pour boiling water to cover peas; let stand 3 to 4 minutes; drain well. Add to hot noodles with salmon and green onions. Stir together mayonnaise, sour cream, lemon juice and Worcestershire sauce. Pour over noodle mixture; gently stir to combine. Bake in preheated 350° oven for 30 minutes or until thoroughly heated. Garnish with lemon wedges and parsley. Serves four.

SALMON NOODLE CASSEROLE

1 can (15 ½ ounces) salmon
3 tablespoons butter or margarine
2 tablespoons flour
½ teaspoon dry mustard
1 tall can (13 ounces) evaporated milk
1 package (10 ounces) mixed vegetables, thawed
and drained
3 cups wide or medium noodles, cooked
1 ½ cups Cheddar cheese, shredded and divided

Drain salmon; break into large chunks. Melt butter in saucepan; stir in flour and dry mustard. Gradually stir in evaporated milk. Cook and stir over medium heat until slightly thickened. Stir in vegetables, cooked noodles and 1 cup cheese. Gently fold in salmon. Pour into greased 2-quart baking dish. Bake, covered, at 350° for 25 minutes. Sprinkle with remaining ½ cup cheese. Bake uncovered 5 minutes or until cheese melts. Serves six.

SALMON AND NOODLE CASSEROLE

8 ounces egg noodles, uncooked
¼ cup butter or margarine
¼ cup onion, minced
2 tablespoons green pepper, chopped
½ cup soft bread cubes
2 cups salmon, flaked
1 can (10 ½ ounces) condensed cream of celery soup
½ cup milk
2 tablespoons pimento, diced
½ teaspoon lemon rind, grated

Cook noodles according to the directions on package. Drain. Melt butter. Cook onion and green pepper in the melted butter until onion is golden brown and tender. Add bread cubes and mix until well coated.

Put salmon, cooked noodles, celery soup, milk, pimento, and lemon rind in a mixing bowl. Mix lightly.

Turn into 2-quart deep casserole. Arrange the bread mixture over the top and bake in a 350° oven about 30 minutes or until bread cubes are nicely browned. Serves six to eight.

SALMON PASTA

1 can (15 ½ ounces) salmon
2 cups zucchini, thickly sliced and quartered
1 cup green pepper, sliced
½ cup green onion, sliced
1 clove garlic, minced
2 or 3 tablespoons oil
1 cup frozen peas, thawed
¼ cup parsley, chopped
1 teaspoon basil, crushed
12 to 16 ounces hot, drained spaghetti or fettuccine
¾ cup to 1 cup heavy cream
Salt and pepper

Drain salmon; break into chunks. Saute zucchini, green pepper, onion and garlic in oil 2 minutes or until crisp-tender. Add salmon, peas, parsley and basil; heat thoroughly. Toss hot pasta with cream; salt and pepper to taste. Toss salmon mixture with pasta. Serve with grated Parmesan cheese. Serves six to eight.

CREAMY SALMON AND PASTA

1 can (15 ½ ounces) salmon
2 tablespoons shallots or onions, minced
2 tablespoons olive oil
Heavy cream
1 teaspoon Dijon mustard
⅛ teaspoon tarragon, crushed
8 ounces large pasta twists, cooked and drained
4 cups lightly packed sliced spinach, thawed and squeezed dry
Parmesan cheese, grated
Salt and pepper

Drain salmon, reserving liquid; break into large chunks. In large skillet, saute shallots in olive oil until tender. Add cream to reserved salmon liquid to equal one cup. Add to skillet with mustard and tarragon; cook over medium heat two minutes or until slightly thickened. Add pasta, spinach and ¼ cup Parmesan cheese; toss gently. Stir in salmon. Season with salt and pepper to taste; heat thoroughly. Serve with additional Parmesan cheese if desired. Serves six.

PASTA AND SALMON

8 ounces spinach noodles, cooked and drained
2 tablespoons butter or margarine
1 can (4 ounces) sliced mushrooms, well-drained
1 can (6 ½ ounces) boneless, skinless salmon, drained and flaked
½ cup grated Parmesan cheese
½ teaspoon ground nutmeg
1 cup sour cream
Paprika

Leave hot noodles in colander while melting butter in cooking pot. Add mushrooms, salmon, cheese and nutmeg. Heat gently over low heat; add noodles, stirring gently until hot. Fold in sour cream; heat just until hot. Sprinkle with paprika and serve immediately. Serves four.

BAKED MACARONI AND SALMON

1 cup cooked macaroni
1 cup canned salmon
1 tablespoon melted butter
1 tablespoon flour
1 cup milk
1 teaspoon salt
Dash of pepper
1 teaspoon onion, chopped
1 teaspoon green pepper, chopped
¼ cup grated American cheese

Combine above ingredients and place in greased casserole dish. Stir together the following topping and sprinkle over casserole:
2 tablespoons melted butter
¼ cup cracker crumbs
Bake in 350° oven for one hour. Serves four.

SALMON NOODLE FRY

1 can (15 ½ ounces) salmon
8 ounces vermicelli or other fine noodles
2 tablespoons white wine vinegar
1 tablespoon cornstarch
5 tablespoons oil
1 clove garlic, minced
2 cups bean sprouts
1 cup green pepper, thinly and vertically sliced
½ cup green onion, diagonally sliced
1 tablespoon lime juice
1 teaspoon lime peel, grated
½ teaspoon sugar
¼ teaspoon red chilies, crushed
Salt and pepper
1 lime, sliced paper-thin

Drain salmon; break into large chunks. Cook vermicelli according to package directions; drain. Combine salmon, vinegar and cornstarch; let stand 15 minutes. Saute salmon in two tablespoons oil in skillet; remove from skillet. Heat one tablespoon oil and garlic. Saute bean sprouts, green pepper and green onion until crisp-tender; remove from skillet. Pan-fry noodles in two tablespoons oil; season with lime juice and peel. Gently stir in salmon, vegetable mixture, sugar, chilies and salt and pepper to taste. Garnish with lime slices. Serves four to six.

SALMON
WITH GREEN FETTUCCINE

1 can (15 ½ ounces) salmon
Milk
¼ cup onion, finely chopped
1 ½ cups mushrooms, sliced
3 tablespoons butter or margarine
¼ cup flour
¼ cup dry white wine
Parmesan cheese, grated
2 tablespoons minced parsley
1 teaspoon dillweed, crushed
Salt and pepper
¾ pound spinach or egg fettuccine noodles, cooked and drained

Drain salmon, reserving liquid; break into large chunks. Add milk to reserved liquid to measure 1¾ cups. Saute onion and mushrooms in butter until onion is tender. Add flour; cook and stir on low heat until blended. Remove from heat; add milk mixture and wine. Heat and stir until mixture comes to a boil; simmer 2 minutes. Carefully stir in salmon, ¼ cup Parmesan cheese, parsley and dill. Season to taste with salt and pepper. Heat, stirring gently, 5 minutes or until thoroughly heated. Serve over hot spinach fettuccine. Serves six.

SALMON
AND SHELLS CASSEROLE

1 can (15 ½ ounces) salmon
1 can (10 ¾ ounces) condensed cream of mushroom soup
1 soup-can water
2 cups uncooked small pasta shells
2 ribs celery, sliced thin
1 tablespoon lemon juice or sherry
1 cup seasoned dry bread crumbs
2 tablespoons butter or margarine, melted
Paprika (optional)

Drain salmon, reserving liquid; set salmon aside.
Add enough water to salmon liquid to make 1 cup.
Pour into 3-quart casserole. Add soup and water; mix
well. Stir in shells, salmon (broken in chunks), celery,
and lemon juice. Mix bread crumbs and butter; sprinkle over top. Sprinkle with paprika. Bake in preheated 350° oven 1 hour or until shells are tender.
Serves four.

BAKED SALMON AND RICE

2 cups cooked rice
2 cups thin white sauce, seasoned with ¼ teaspoon Worcestershire sauce
1 can salmon, drained and flaked
½ cup buttered bread crumbs

Line the bottom of a greased 1½-quart baking dish
with rice. Then layer white sauce and salmon alter-
natively, ending with sauce. Cover with crumbs.
Bake at 350° about 20 minutes or until crumbs are
browned. Serves four.

SALMON-RICE CASSEROLE

½ cup milk
½ pound processed pimento cheese
1 teaspoon salt
¼ teaspoon ground black pepper
3 cups cooked rice
1 cup salmon, flaked
¼ cup stuffed olives, chopped
Sliced stuffed olives for garnish

Combine milk, cheese, salt, and pepper in a double boiler. Heat only until well blended and smooth.

Put a layer of cooked rice in a well-greased 1½-quart casserole. On top of this arrange layers of salmon, chopped olives, and the cheese sauce. Repeat, ending with cheese sauce. Arrange slices of stuffed olives around edge for garnish.

Bake in a 350° oven about 30 minutes or until golden-browned. Serves six.

SALMON-RICE MEDLEY

3 (11-ounce) packages frozen rice with peas and mushrooms
¾ cup onion, chopped
2 tablespoons butter or margarine
2 cloves garlic, crushed
¾ teaspoons curry powder
1 (15½-ounce) can salmon
2 hard-cooked eggs
⅛ teaspoon cayenne pepper

Prepare rice medley according to package directions. Saute onion in butter with garlic and curry powder. Drain salmon and break into chunks. Chop eggs, reserving a few slices for garnish. In 8-inch-square baking dish, combine eggs, salmon, rice, pepper and onion mixture. Cover and bake at 350° for 15 to 20 minutes or until thoroughly heated. Serves four to six.

SEAFOOD VEGETABLE COMBO

1 can (7¾ ounces) salmon
1 package (10 ounces) frozen cut Italian beans
or Chinese pea pods
½ cup each julienned carrot and celery
2 tablespoons chopped onion
1 tablespoon oil
2 tablespoons dry white wine
¼ teaspoon oregano, crushed
Dash hot pepper sauce
Salt
½ cup shrimp

Drain salmon; break into large chunks. Microwave frozen green beans until tender. Combine carrot, celery, onion and oil in 1½-quart microwave-proof dish; cover loosely with waxed paper or plastic wrap vented by folding back one corner. Microwave at high two minutes; add wine, oregano and hot pepper sauce. Salt to taste. Add beans and seafood; microwave, covered, at medium (50 percent power) for two minutes or until all ingredients are thoroughly heated. Serves four to six. Serve with cooked rice.

BAKED SALMON
WITH CUCUMBER DILL SAUCE

1 can (15½ ounces) salmon, drained and flaked
1 medium-size onion, chopped
1 small sweet green pepper, halved, seeded and chopped
½ cup celery, chopped
½ cup plain dry bread crumbs
¼ cup plain yogurt
¼ cup mayonnaise
1 egg, slightly beaten
¼ teaspoon pepper
Cucumber Dill Sauce (recipes follows)

Preheat oven to 325°. Generously grease four 6-ounce custard cups. Combine salmon, onion, green pepper, celery, bread crumbs, yogurt, mayonnaise, egg and pepper in bowl. Stir until well blended. Divide mixture evenly among prepared custard cups; pack well. Arrange on small cookie sheet. Bake in preheated slow oven (325°) for 30 minutes or until salmon mixture begins to pull away from sides of cups. To unmold, run small knife around edge of each cup. Invert onto serving dish. Spoon Cucumber Dill Sauce over tops. Garnish with sprigs of dill, if you wish. Serves four.

Cucumber Dill Sauce:
Stir together ½ cup mayonnaise, ¼ cup sour cream, ¼ cup plain yogurt, ¾ cup finely chopped seeded cucumber, ¼ cup finely chopped onion and 1 tablespoon chopped fresh dill, or 1 teaspoon dillweed, in saucepan. Heat over very low heat just until warmed through.

RAGOUT OF SALMON AND TOMATOES

1 medium-sized onion, chopped
1 medium-sized green pepper, cleaned and minced
2 tablespoons butter or margarine
3 tablespoons flour
1 cup milk
1 can tomatoes, undrained
½ teaspoon crumbled dried oregano or thyme
Salt and pepper to taste
1 can (15½ ounces) salmon, drained and flaked

In a large saucepan, saute the onion and green pepper in the butter until the onion is tender. Mix in the flour and cook 1 minute. Gradually add the milk and the liquid of the tomatoes, stirring constantly. Cook slowly, stirring until thickened and smooth. Add the tomatoes and break up with a spoon or fork. Add the oregano, salt and pepper and cook slowly, being careful not to boil, for 10 minutes. Mix in the salmon and cook another 5 minutes. Serves four to six.

SALMON BUNDLES

1 cup green onion, sliced
2 tablespoons butter or margarine
1 8-ounce can water chestnuts, drained and chopped
½ cup sour cream
1 2-ounce jar sliced pimento, drained and chopped
¼ cup fine dry bread crumbs
1 beaten egg
½ cup shredded American cheese (2 ounces)
¼ teaspoon pepper
1 can (15½ ounces) salmon, drained and flaked
2 packages (8 each) refrigerated crescent rolls
Shredded American cheese or sour cream

In saucepan cook the onion in butter or margarine until tender. Remove from heat. Stir in water chestnuts, sour cream, pimento, bread crumbs, egg, cheese, and pepper. Stir in fish.

Unroll dough; form into eight 6-inch by 4-inch rectangles, using two rolls to form one rectangle; seal perforations. Spoon 1/3 cup filling on each. Fold dough over to seal; seal with tines of fork. Place on ungreased baking sheet. Bake in a 425° oven 10 minutes or until golden brown. To serve, top each with additional shredded cheese or sour cream. Makes 8 sandwiches.

SALMON-STUFFED FILLETS WITH BERNAISE SAUCE

1 can (15½ ounces) salmon, drained
1 egg
½ cup parsley, chopped
½ teaspoon salt
Pepper to taste
1 envelope (⅞ ounce) Hollandaise sauce mix, prepared as directed
4 6-ounce fillets of sole or flounder, halved lengthwise
2 tablespoons butter or margarine, melted
3 tablespoons dry white wine
½ teaspoon dried tarragon
Orange slices for garnish

In food processor or blender process salmon, egg, parsley, salt, pepper and ¼ cup Hollandaise sauce until blended. Spread stuffing on darker side of each fillet half. Roll up; secure with wooden pick if necessary. Place rolls upright in shallow baking dish: drizzle with butter. Bake in preheated 375[DEGREES] oven 15 minutes until fish flakes easily when tested with fork. Discard wooden picks. Meanwhile, stirring occasionally, cook wine, tarragon and remaining Hollandaise in small saucepan over low heat 5 minutes to blend flavors. Serve with stuffed fillets garnished with orange slices. Serves four.

CASSEROLE ALASKA

4 slices of bread, buttered
1 can (7¾ ounces) salmon, flaked
1 egg
1½ cups milk
Salt and pepper

Butter 4 slices of bread, cut or break into cubes.

Flake salmon, combine with bread in buttered casserole.

Beat one egg slightly, add to 1 ½ cups milk, season with salt and pepper. Pour over bread and salmon and bake in moderate oven, 350° for 25 to 30 minutes. Serves three.

SALMON AND POTATO CASSEROLE

4 potatoes, peeled and sliced thin
3 tablespoons flour
Salt and pepper
1 can (15½ ounces) salmon, drained and flaked
1 medium onion, chopped
2 eggs, beaten
1 tablespoon butter
2 cups scalded milk
Nutmeg

Put half of potatoes in casserole. Sprinkle with half the flour, salt and pepper. Cover with half the salmon. Sprinkle with half the onion. Repeat layers in same order.

Gradually add beaten eggs to scalded milk; stir well. Pour over potatoes and salmon. Sprinkle with nutmeg.

Bake or put in crockpot for 7 to 10 hours on low. Serves four.

HERBED SALMON BAKE

1 cup chicken broth
1 can (15½ ounces) salmon, drained and flaked
2 cups seasoned stuffing croutons
1 cup grated cheddar cheese
2 eggs, beaten
¼ teaspoon dry mustard

Combine all ingredients; mix well. Put in greased pan. Bake at 350° for 25 to 30 minutes. Serves four.

SALMON WITH SOUR CREAM AND DILL TOPPING

1 can (15½ ounces) salmon, undrained
4 baked-potato skins
½ cup sour cream
Minced dill or green onions to taste

Place salmon in saucepan; heat gently. Drain; break salmon in chunks; spoon into potato skins; top with sour cream; sprinkle with dill. Serves four.

SALMON DIVAN

1 package frozen broccoli
½ tablespoon butter
½ tablespoon flour
½ teaspoon salt
Pinch of pepper
½ cup skim milk
2 tablespoons American cheese, grated
1 small can tomatoes, drained
1 can (7¾ ounces) salmon, drained
1 tablespoon cornflakes, crushed

Preheat oven to 375°. Cook the broccoli as directed on the package. Drain and place in baking dish. Melt the butter in a saucepan, blend in the flour, salt, and pepper. Gradually add the milk, stirring constantly, until it boils. Simmer for 5 minutes. Stir in the cheese and tomatoes. Break the salmon in pieces and place on the broccoli. Pour the sauce over, sprinkle with cornflakes. Place in oven and bake for 30 minutes. Serves four.

CREAMED SALMON
IN BISCUIT RING

1 can (15½ ounces) salmon, drained and coarsely flaked
1 can (10½ ounces) condensed cream of mushroom soup, undiluted
1 cup frozen peas, thawed
1 cup milk
2 tablespoons dry sherry
¼ teaspoon salt
1 (8-ounce) container refrigerated biscuits (10 biscuits)
2 tablespoons melted butter or margarine
2 teaspoons dried parsley flakes

Heat oven to 425°. In a large bowl, gently combine salmon, soup, peas, milk, sherry, and salt. Pour mixture into an ungreased deep 2-quart casserole. Open biscuit container according to label directions and separate biscuits. Brush melted butter over tops of biscuits and sprinkle with parsley. Arrange biscuits in a ring with sides touching on top of the salmon mixture. Bake, uncovered, 15 to 20 minutes, or until mixture is bubbling and the biscuits are golden brown. Serves four.

SCALLOPED SALMON

1 1/3 cups packaged seasoned bread stuffing
1/3 cup melted butter or margarine
1 can (15½ ounces) salmon
3 hard-cooked eggs, chopped
1 can (10½ ounces) condensed cream of mushroom soup, undiluted
1 tablespoon instant minced onion
1 tablespoon dried parsley flakes

Heat oven to 400°. Grease a shallow 1-quart baking dish with shortening. Combine bread stuffing and butter in a medium-sized bowl. Set aside 1/3 cup of the mixture. Drain liquid from salmon and reserve. Remove skin and bones from salmon and flake coarsely. Add enough water to salmon liquid to make ¾ cup. Combine the 1-cup crumb mixture with the salmon, salmon liquid, eggs, soup, onion, and parsley flakes. Spoon into prepared baking dish. Sprinkle with reserved crumbs. Bake, uncovered, 20 minutes. Serves four to six.

SALMON
WITH CORN BREAD TOPPING

1 can (15½ ounces) salmon
2 cans (10½-ounce) condensed cream of mushroom soup, undiluted
¼ cup milk
1 (10-ounce) package frozen peas, cooked and drained
1 (12-ounce) package corn muffin mix
¼ teaspoon salt
½ teaspoon celery seed
¼ teaspoon ground thyme
½ teaspoon instant minced onion
1 egg
1/3 cup milk
2 whole canned pimentos, chopped
¼ cup finely chopped green pepper

Heat oven to 400°. Drain liquid from salmon and reserve. Remove skin and bones from salmon. Combine soup, liquid from salmon, and the ¼ cup milk in a saucepan; heat over moderate heat until boiling. Remove pan from heat. Break salmon into chunks and add to soup mixture along with cooked peas. Pour into ungreased shallow 2½-quart casserole. Combine corn muffin mix, salt, celery seed, thyme, and onion in a medium-sized bowl. Combine egg and the 1/3 cup milk in a cup; add to muffin mix and combine thoroughly. Stir in pimento and green pepper. Drop by spoonfuls over hot mixture in casserole. Bake, uncovered, 30 minutes, or until mixture bubbles at the edges and topping is lightly browned. Serves six.

SALMON
AND GREEN CHILI STRATA

6 slices firm white bread, lightly buttered
3 cups sharp cheddar cheese, shredded
4 ounces green chilies, diced
1 can (15½ ounces) salmon
4 eggs
2 cups milk
1 teaspoon salt
1 teaspoon prepared horseradish
¼ teaspoon pepper

Lightly butter one side of bread; cut into ½-inch cubes. Have ready cheese, green chilies, and salmon.

Sprinkle half the bread cubes in a greased shallow 2 ½-quart baking dish; top evenly with half of the cheese, then half of the chilies. Arrange fish evenly over chilies. Top with remaining bread cubes, then cheese, then chilies.

In a bowl, beat together eggs, milk, salt, prepared horseradish, and pepper; pour over casserole. Cover and chill at least 8 hours or overnight.

Bake, uncovered, in a 350° oven for about 50 minutes or until top is puffy and richly golden. Let stand 10 to 15 minutes before serving. Serves six to eight.

SALMON AND BROCCOLI CASSEROLE

2 tablespoons butter
1 tablespoon flour
1 teaspoon salt
¾ teaspoon white pepper
1 cup skim milk
1 cup tomatoes, peeled and chopped
2 packages frozen broccoli, half-cooked and drained
1 can (15½ ounces) salmon, drained and flaked
2 tablespoons dry bread crumbs

Melt 1 tablespoon margarine in a saucepan; blend in the flour, salt and pepper. Add the milk, stirring steadily to the boiling point. Stir in the tomatoes; cook over low heat 5 minutes.

Spread the broccoli on the bottom of a 2-quart casserole or baking dish. Cover with the salmon and pour the sauce over all. Sprinkle with the bread crumbs and dot with the remaining margarine. Bake in a 375° oven 30 minutes. Serves six.

SALMON CASSEROLE

1 can salmon, flaked
1 can mushrooms, sliced and drained
1 can baby lima beans, drained
1 can cream of mushroom soup
Salt and pepper
2 tablespoons parsley, chopped

Combine first 4 ingredients in a buttered shallow casserole and season to taste. Heat to boiling in a moderately hot 375° Oven. Serve sprinkled with parsley. Serves four.

SALMON CASSEROLE

1 cup (firmly packed) soft bread crumbs, grated
½ cup rich milk
¼ cup dry white table wine
1 can salmon, drained, boned, and flaked
1 cup Cheddar cheese, grated
2 eggs, slightly beaten
1 tablespoon lemon juice
½ teaspoon grated lemon peel
2 tablespoons onion, grated
½ teaspoon Worcestershire sauce
Salt, celery salt, garlic salt, and pepper to taste
½ cup buttered fine bread crumbs

Soak soft bread crumbs in milk for 10 minutes; beat well with a fork. Add all remaining ingredients except buttered crumbs; mix well. Turn into a greased baking dish; top with buttered crumbs. Bake in a moderate oven (350°) for 30 to 40 minutes or until firm in the center. Serve with wedges of lemon. Serves four or five.

SALMON SANDWICH BAKE

12 slices sandwich bread
¼ cup soft butter or margarine
2 teaspoons prepared mustard
2 cans (7¾ ounces each) salmon, drained
1 cup Cheddar cheese, shredded
¼ cup pimento-stuffed olives, sliced
1 small onion, chopped (about ¼ cup)
1 package (10 ounces) frozen green peas
1 can (10¾ ounces) condensed cream of shrimp soup
¼ cup milk
Dill pickles

Toast bread; trim crusts. Mix butter and mustard; spread over 1 side of each bread slice. Arrange 6 slices bread buttered-sides up in ungreased baking dish, 11¾ inches by 7½ inches by 1¾ inches.

Heat oven to 350°. Flake salmon, removing skin and bones. Mix salmon, cheese, olives and onions. Spread salmon mixture evenly over bread in baking dish. Cut remaining 6 slices bread diagonally in half; place buttered sides up on salmon mixture. Rinse frozen peas under running cold water to separate; layer on bread. Mix soup and milk; pour evenly on and around sandwiches. Bake uncovered until hot and bubbly, 25 to 30 minutes. Serve with dill pickles. Serves six.

PEPPER-BAKED SALMON

2 cans (7¾ ounces each) salmon, flaked
¼ teaspoon onion juice
1½ cups bread crumbs
2 tablespoons butter, melted
¼ cup milk
4 bell peppers, halved
Salt and pepper

Salt and pepper flaked salmon to taste; add onion juice, then mix well. Add bread crumbs and melted butter.

Stir in enough milk to make the mixture fairly moist and parboil for 5 minutes. Take 4 bell peppers (depending on size, but this mixture should be just right for 4 fairly large peppers) and cut them in half lengthwise. Remove and discard the seeds, and parboil for 5 minutes.

Fill peppers with the salmon mixture. Place in a baking pan, pour in a little boiling water (to prevent sticking) and bake for 15 to 20 minutes in moderate oven, or until peppers are soft but not broken. Remove and place on serving plate. Serves four.

SALMON TORTILLA BAKE

6 corn tortillas
Oil
1 can (7¾ ounces) salmon
½ cup onion, chopped
2 cans (4 ounces each) green chilies, diced
½ cup Half-and-Half
½ cup tomato sauce
1 ½ cups (about ¼ pound) Monterey Jack cheese, shredded

Cut tortillas into half-inch strips. Fry a few at a time in half an inch hot oil until crisp but not browned. Drain on paper towels. Drain salmon, reserving one tablespoon liquid; flake.

Saute onion in one tablespoon oil; add chilies, Half-and-Half, tomato sauce and reserved salmon liquid. In a greased 9-inch round baking dish, layer half of tortilla strips, half of onion mixture, half of salmon and half of cheese; repeat layers.

Bake at 350° for 30 minutes or until thoroughly heated. Serves four.

SALMON SPINACH BAKE

2 cups baking mix
½ cup cold water
1 teaspoon grated lemon peel
1 package (10 ounces) frozen chopped spinach, thawed and well-drained
1 package (8 ounces) cream cheese, softened
1 teaspoon poultry seasoning
2 teaspoons diced pimento
1 teaspoon lemon juice
1 cup thinly sliced mushrooms (about 4 ounces) or 1 can (4 ounces) sliced mushrooms, drained
1 can (15½ ounces) salmon, drained and flaked

Heat oven to 400°. Lightly grease square pan, 9 inches by 9 inches by 2 inches. Mix baking mix, water and lemon peel with fork until soft dough forms. Turn dough onto cloth covered board lightly floured with baking mix. Knead five times. Divide dough into halves. Roll one half into 9-inch square; place in pan. Mix remaining ingredients; spread over dough in pan. Roll remaining dough into 9-inch square; place over mixture in pan. Press lightly onto filling and sides of pan. Bake until golden brown, 25 to 30 minutes. Serves four.

SALMON CASSEROLE

5 medium potatoes
1 can (15½ ounces) salmon
Salt and pepper to taste
1 egg, slightly beaten
1 tablespoon flour
1 teaspoon chopped parsley
1 cup milk
Bread crumbs (flavored preferred)
3 tablespoons butter

Peel potatoes, slice thin and place in salted water. Boil for two minutes. Skin and bone the salmon. Arrange the potatoes and salmon in layers in a buttered casserole dish, first a layer of potatoes, then a layer of salmon sprinkled with salt, pepper and little chunks of butter; then potatoes, then the rest of the salmon, then the remaining potatoes. Salt again sparingly.

In a separate bowl, mix the egg, milk, flour, and parsley. Pour this mixture over the potatoes and salmon, making sure it covers the whole casserole. Top with flavored bread crumbs and dabs of butter.

Bake in a 325° oven for 35 minutes. Serve with melted butter. Serves four.

SALMON CASSEROLE
WITH OLIVE SAUCE

2 cans (16 ounces each) salmon
6 slices fresh bread, shredded
2 eggs, well beaten
1 cup milk
2 tablespoons parsley, snipped
¼ cup onion, minced
1 teaspoon salt
1 tablespoon Worcestershire sauce
¼ teaspoon poultry seasoning
¼ cup butter or margarine, melted
¼ cup lemon juice

Olive Sauce:
2 tablespoons butter or margarine
2 tablespoons flour
½ teaspoon salt
⅛ teaspoon ground black pepper
1 cup milk
½ cup stuffed olives, sliced

Combine all ingredients up to and including lemon juice. Turn into a greased 1½-quart casserole. Bake in a 350° oven for 50 to 60 minutes or until firm in center. Take hot from oven to table. Serves eight.

Olive Sauce:
Melt butter in saucepan. Remove from heat. Add flour, salt and pepper. Stir until smooth. Slowly add milk, stirring to avoid lumps. Cook over low direct heat, stirring constantly, until smooth and thickened, about five minutes. Add sliced olives. Pour into sauce bowl for serving with Salmon Casserole.

SALMON SOUFFLE

1 cup medium cream sauce
2 tablespoons parsley, minced
¼ teaspoon Worcestershire sauce
1 tablespoon sherry wine
Onion juice to taste
2 eggs, separated
1 can (15½ ounces) salmon, drained and flaked

Prepare cream sauce. Mix in parsley, Worcestershire, sherry and onion juice. Remove from heat immediately and add beaten egg yolks. Return to heat and cook 1 minute. Gently fold in flaked salmon followed by the stiffly beaten egg whites. Pour into greased 1½-quart baking dish. Bake at 350° for 45 minutes. Serves four.

FISH SOUFFLE

2 cups canned salmon, boned, skinned and flaked
¼ teaspoon salt
⅛ teaspoon paprika
2 teaspoons lemon juice

Cook together 5 minutes.

½ cup dry bread crumbs
½ cup milk

Add the fish and:
3 egg yolks, beaten thick

Fold in:
3 egg whites, beaten stiff

Spoon into a buttered baking dish. Set in a pan of hot water and bake at 350° until firm (about 30 minutes). Serve with Hollandaise sauce. Serves four.

CHEESE-SOUFFLED SALMON AND VEGETABLES

1 package (10-ounce) frozen asparagus or broccoli spears
1 can (15½ ounces) salmon, drained, bones and
skin removed, broken into pieces
2/3 cup mayonnaise or salad dressing
2/3 cup (3 ounces) shredded or grated cheese
½ teaspoon finely shredded lemon peel
4 egg whites
¼ teaspoon cream of tartar
¼ teaspoon salt
2 tablespoons sliced almonds
Lemon wedges

Cook asparagus or broccoli according to package
directions until crisp-tender; drain. Arrange vegetables in the bottom of an ungreased 12-inch by 7½-inch
by 2-inch baking dish or 4 individual baking dishes.
Sprinkle salmon atop vegetable.

In mixing bowl, combine mayonnaise or salad
dressing, cheese and lemon peel. In large mixer bowl,
beat egg whites, cream of tartar, and salt on high
speed of electric mixer to stiff peaks. Fold in mayonnaise mixture. Spread over fish and vegetables.
Sprinkle with sliced almonds. Bake in 350° oven
about 20 minutes or until knife inserted in souffle
layer near center comes out clean. Serve immediately
with lemon wedges. Serves four.

SALMON SOUFFLE

1 can (7¾ ounces) salmon, drained and flaked
1 small zucchini (6 ounces), shredded
1 celery stalk, finely chopped
1 small green onion, minced
1½ teaspoons lemon juice
¼ teaspoon salt
Mayonnaise
2 egg whites, at room temperature
2 ounces Cheddar cheese, shredded (½ cup)
⅛ teaspoon ground red pepper
4 slices whole-wheat bread
About 12 medium spinach leaves

About 30 minutes before serving: in medium bowl, stir salmon, zucchini, celery, green onion, lemon juice, salt, and 3 tablespoons mayonnaise until blended.

In small bowl with mixer at high speed, beat egg whites until stiff peaks form. Gently fold shredded cheese, ground red pepper, and ¼ cup mayonnaise into beaten egg whites.

Place bread slices on cookie sheet; toast bread 1 to 2 minutes on each side in broiler until lightly golden; remove from broiler. On each toast slice, arrange some spinach leaves. Spoon salmon mixture on spinach; top with egg-white mixture; broil 1 to 2 minutes until egg-white mixture is lightly browned. Serves four.

SALMON SCRAMBLE

2 tablespoons butter or margarine
½ cup onion, chopped
1 can (7¾ ounces) salmon, drained
2 teaspoons oyster sauce
6 eggs, slightly beaten
Salt and pepper

Heat the butter in a frying pan over medium heat; add the onion and cook until limp.

Discard skin and bones from canned salmon; add salmon and oyster sauce to onion and cook, stirring gently, until salmon is hot. Reduce heat to low, pour in eggs, and cook, lifting set portion to allow uncooked egg to flow underneath.

When eggs are cooked to your liking, remove from heat and slide onto a serving platter. Add salt and pepper to taste. Serves four.

SALMON AND EGGS

8 slices bacon
1 medium onion, chopped
1 can (7¾ ounces) salmon, drained and flaked
6-8 eggs, beaten
Salt and pepper

Fry bacon until crisp. Remove from pan. Pour off all but 3 tablespoons dripping. Saute onion in dripping. Add salmon to frying pan. When salmon is well heated, add eggs, salt and pepper. Stir constantly until eggs are cooked. Serve with bacon and home fries. Serves four to six.

SALMON DILL OMELET
WITH SOUR CREAM

8 eggs
¼ cup water
1 teaspoon salt
¼ teaspoon pepper
¼ cup dill, chopped
2 tablespoons butter or margarine
1 can (15½ ounces) salmon, drained and flaked
1 cup sour cream
Dill sprigs for garnish

Whisk eggs, water, salt, pepper and chopped dill in medium-size bowl until blended. Slowly heat omelet pan or 8- or 9-inch non-stick skillet until hot. For each omelet add ½ tablespoon butter; heat until sizzling but not brown. Add ½ cup egg mixture; cook, tilting pan so bottom is covered, until omelet starts to set. Run spatula around edges to lift cooked portions and let uncooked egg run under. Continue until omelet is almost dry and top and bottom is golden. Place 2 tablespoons salmon and sour cream on omelet; fold in half over filling; slide onto serving plate. Top with 2 tablespoons each salmon and sour cream; garnish with dill sprig. Serves four.

LEMON SALMON OMELET

6 eggs, separated
Grated peel and juice of half fresh lemon
⅛ teaspoon cream of tartar
1 can (7¾ ounces) salmon, drained and flaked
2 tablespoons butter
2 tablespoons butter
2 tablespoons flour
1 tablespoon green onion, sliced
Grated peel of ½ fresh lemon
½ teaspoon dried dill weed
¼ teaspoon salt
Dash pepper
1 cup milk

In small bowl, beat egg yolks, lemon peel and juice of half lemon until thick and light colored.

With clean egg beater, beat egg whites until foamy; add cream of tartar and continue beating until stiff but not dry. Fold in egg yolks and salmon. In oven-proof 10-inch skillet, melt butter; pour in egg mixture. Cook over medium heat for 5 minutes or until underside is lightly browned. Then place in oven heated to 325°. Bake at 325° for 10 minutes or until top is set.

Loosen around edges with spatula. Make slit across center; fold in half. Carefully turn out onto warmed serving dish. Serve with Dill Sauce. Serves three to four.

Dill Sauce:
In saucepan, melt butter. Remove from heat; stir or whisk in flour, green onion, lemon peel, dill, salt and pepper. Gradually add milk. Cook over medium heat, stirring until thickened. Makes 1 1/3 cup sauce.

SALMON VEGETABLE STEW WITH BASIL SAUCE

1 can (15½-ounce) salmon
1 cup each celery and onion, chopped
2 cloves garlic, minced
1 tablespoon olive oil or oil
Water
¼ teaspoon salt
1 small russett potato, pared and diced
1 cup cut green beans
2 leeks, thinly sliced
2 tablespoons small macaroni
1 zucchini, thinly sliced
1 cup shredded spinach or cabbage
½ cup frozen peas, thawed
1 tablespoon cornstarch
Basil Sauce (recipe follows)

Drain salmon, reserving 2 tablespoons liquid; chunk. Saute celery, onion and garlic in oil in large kettle 10 minutes or until golden. Add 1 quart water, reserved salmon liquid and salt. Bring to boil; simmer, covered, 30 minutes. Add potato; simmer, covered, 5 minutes. Add beans, leeks, macaroni and zucchini; simmer, covered, 5 minutes. Add reserved salmon, spinach and peas. Simmer, uncovered, 5 minutes or until salmon is thoroughly heated and vegetables are crisp-tender. Combine cornstarch and 2 tablespoons water. Add to soup; cook and stir until slighly thickened and clear. Serve with Basil Sauce. Serves six.

Basil Sauce:
3 tablespoons olive or vegetable oil
3 tablespoons butter or margarine
2 tablespoons lemon juice
¼ cup parsley, chopped
2 tablespoons basil, crushed
½ cup Parmesan cheese

In a food processor or blender, combine oil and margarine, lemon juice, chopped parsley and crushed basil, process until smooth. Add Parmesan cheese and process until well blended. Makes about 2 to 3 cups.

STEWED SALMON

6-8 slices bacon
1 medium onion, chopped
1 can salmon, flaked
8-10 drops of Red Devil or Tabasco sauce
½ teaspoon salt
¼ teaspoon black pepper
1 cup water
Rice

Fry bacon. Remove from pan and reserve. Add onions to the pan. Fry them in the bacon drippings until golden. Add salmon and remaining ingredients. Simmer, uncovered, for 5-10 minutes to blend flavors. Serve hot with rice and bacon. Serves four.

SALMON BISQUE

2 tablespoons butter or margarine
½ cup onion, chopped
2 tablespoons flour
4 cups milk, divided
2 cans (7¾ ounces each) salmon, drained and flaked fine

In medium saucepan heat butter; add onion; cook until tender but not browned. Stir in flour, then 2/3 cup milk until smooth. Bring to boil, stirring constantly. Gradually stir in remaining milk and the salmon. Cook until slightly thickened. Serves six.

SALMON VEGETABLE CHOWDER

1 can (10½ ounces) condensed chicken broth
2 2/3 cups water
1 10-ounce package frozen succotash
1 cup celery, chopped
½ cup onion, chopped
½ cup wheat berries
1 8-ounce package cream cheese, cut into cubes
1 can (15½ ounces) salmon, drained, skin and
bones removed, coarsely flaked

In a 3½-quart electric crockery cooker, combine first
6 ingredients. Cover; cook on low-heat setting for 8 to
10 hours (or high-heat setting for 3½ to 4 hours). Turn
cooker to high-heat setting. Add cheese, stirring until
melted. Stir in salmon. Cover; cook 10 minutes more.
Serves four.

SALMON CHOWDER

1 can (7¾ ounces) salmon, flaked
1 can peas
2 cans cream of celery soup
1 cup milk
1 can cream of mushroom soup
6 stuffed olives, chopped
3 tablespoons onion, chopped
3 tablespoons parsley, chopped
1 tablespoon capers
Salt and pepper

Combine all ingredients, heat to boiling and serve.
If a thinner soup is preferred, add milk to taste. Serves
four to six.

SALMON CORN CHOWDER

¼ cup butter or margarine
1 large onion, chopped
1 cup celery, diced
1 clove garlic, minced
2 tablespoons all-purpose flour
3½ cups chicken broth
2 cups Half-and-Half
1 can (17 ounces) cream-style corn
½ teaspoon salt, or to taste
¼ teaspoon white pepper
1 can (15½ ounces) salmon, drained and flaked
Parsley, chopped for garnish (optional)

Melt butter in large heavy saucepan over medium heat. Add onion, celery and garlic; cook 4 to 5 minutes until onion is translucent. Stir in flour until blended. Gradually stir in 1 cup broth. Stir until boiling and thickened. Stir in remaining broth, the Half-and-Half, corn, salt and pepper. Simmer uncovered 15 minutes, but do not boil. Remove from heat; add salmon. Garnish each serving with parsley. Makes 8 cups.

SALMON CHOWDER

1 1/3 cups instant non-fat dry milk
1 quart water
1 can (7¾ ounces) salmon
½ cup celery
¼ cup dry onion soup mix
½ can (cup) condensed tomato soup (undiluted)
1 teaspoon salt
3 tablespoons margarine
2/3 cup instant potato buds

Melt margarine, add celery and saute until transparent. Dissolve instant milk in water. Add salmon, dry onion soup mix, tomato soup, salt and potato buds. After celery is cooked, add it to mixture and simmer on low heat or in double boiler about 8 to 10 minutes. Serves four to six.

SALMON CHOWDER

4 medium-size potatoes (1¼ pounds), pared and cut into ½-inch thick cubes
1¾ cups water
2 cups milk
½ teaspoon salt
1 package (10 ounces) frozen peas and carrots
1 small onion, finely chopped
1 tablespoon butter
1 tablespoon flour
1 can (15½ ounces) salmon, drained, skin and bones removed
1 teaspoon Worcestershire sauce
2 teaspoons lemon juice
4 drops liquid red pepper seasoning

Combine potatoes, water, ½ cup of the milk and salt in large saucepan. Bring to boil. Lower heat and simmer, uncovered, until potatoes are tender, about 8 minutes. Add mixed vegetables; cover and remove from heat; reserve.

Saute onion in butter in medium-size saucepan until softened, about 2 minutes. Stir in flour; cook 1 minute, stirring. Add remaining milk; cook, stirring, until smooth and thickened, about 5 minutes. Add to potato mixture in large saucepan. Bring gently to boiling. Lower heat. Add salmon, Worcestershire, lemon juice and red pepper seasoning. Stir until heated through. Serves four.

HOT SALMON CHOWDER

1 cup carrots, sliced
1 onion, sliced and divided into rings
2 cans (7¾ ounces each) salmon, flaked
1 large can evaporated milk
½ cup heavy cream
2 cans cream of mushroom soup
¼ cup green pepper, chopped
¼ cup celery, chopped
¼ clove garlic, crushed
1 pinch thyme
2 tablespoons parsley, minced
Salt and pepper to taste

Heat all ingredients to boiling. Serve with hard crackers or hot garlic bread. Serves four to six.

COLD SALMON SOUP

1 can (7¾ ounces) salmon, drained and flaked
½ cup chopped onion
1 tablespoon butter
2 medium cucumbers, peeled, seeded, cubed
1 cup cubed potatoes
1 cup chicken broth
Salt and pepper to taste
1½ tablespoons lemon juice
½ teaspoon dried dill weed
2 cups cream
Lemon wedges
Chopped chives

Drain salmon well. Saute onion in butter until soft. Add cucumbers, potatoes, chicken broth, salt and pepper. Simmer until vegetables are tender, about 10 to 15 minutes. Blend or process until smooth. Add lemon juice and dill. Process 3 seconds. Stir in salmon and cream. Chill. Serve in chilled bowls. Garnish with chives and serve with lemon wedges. Serves four.

POTATO CHEESE SOUP
WITH SALMON

1 large onion, thinly sliced (about 2 cups)
2 ribs celery, diced (about 1 ¼ cups)
¼ cup butter or margarine
4 medium potatoes (about 1 1/3 pound), peeled
and thinly sliced (about 3 ½ cups)
1 cup chicken broth
3 cups milk
1 cup Half and Half
2 cups sharp Cheddar cheese, grated
1 teaspoon thyme
1 tablespoon Worcestershire sauce
1 can (15½ ounces) salmon, broken into chunks
Salt and pepper to taste
2 tablespoons minced fresh parsley

Saute onion and celery in butter until tender. Add potatoes and chicken broth; cook, covered, until potatoes are tender, about 20 minutes. Add 2 cups of the milk. Puree potato mixture and liquid in blender or food processor in several batches. Return to saucepan, add remaining 1 cup milk, the Half and Half, cheese, thyme, Worcestershire sauce and salmon. Season with salt and pepper. Cook stirring, until salmon is hot and cheese is melted. Serve hot garnished with minced fresh parsley. Serves six.

SALMON MOUSSE

2 envelopes unflavored gelatin
1 can (15½ ounces) salmon, drained (reserve liquid)
1 stalk celery, cut into 3-inch pieces
1 small onion, quartered
½ medium cucumber, peeled, seeded and cut into pieces
1 cup (½ pint) whipping or heavy cream
¾ cup mayonnaise
¼ cup lemon juice
1 teaspoon dill weed
½ teaspoon salt

In medium saucepan, sprinkle unflavored gelatin over reserved liquid blended with enough water to equal 1 cup; let stand 1 minute. Stir over low heat until gelatin is completely dissolved, about 5 minutes.

In 5-cup blender or food processor, process gelatin mixture, vegetables, cream, mayonnaise and lemon juice at high speed until blended. Add salmon, dill and salt; process until blended. Pour into 5½ cup mold or bowl; chill until firm. Makes about 5½ cups spread.

BLENDER SALMON MOUSSE

1 envelope plain gelatin
2 tablespoons onions, diced
2 tablespoons lemon juice
½ cup boiling water
½ cup mayonnaise
2 sprigs fresh dill or 1 teaspoon dried
½ teaspoon salt
¼ teaspoon white pepper
2 cans (7¾ ounces each) salmon, drained
1 cup heavy cream
Lemon and cucumber slices for garnish

Combine the gelatin, onions, lemon juice and boiling water in the blender. Blend at high speed for about 30 seconds. Add mayonnaise, dill, salt, pepper and salmon. Turn to high speed for about 20 seconds. Remove blender cover and gradually add the cream until thoroughly blended. Turn into an oiled 1-quart mold. Chill. Turn out carefully. Garnish with slices of lemon and cucumber. Serves eight.

SALMON MOUSSE

2 envelopes unflavored gelatin
Water
2 cans (15½-ounces each) salmon, drained (reserve liquid)
1 cup each mayonnaise and sour cream
¼ cup lemon juice, or to taste
1 teaspoon each salt, paprika and hot-pepper sauce
Lettuce, dill sprigs and lemon wedges for garnish

In small saucepan soften gelatin in ½ cup cold water. Add enough water to salmon liquid to make 1 cup; add to gelatin and stir over medium heat until gelatin dissolves. Cool. In processor or blender, whirl remaining ingredients (except garnish) in two batches until smooth. Blend salmon and gelatin mixtures. Pour into lightly oiled 8-cup mold; cover; chill until set. Unmold on lettuce-lined plate; garnish with dill and lemon.

EASY SALMON MOUSSE

1 envelope unflavored gelatin
¾ cup water
1 cup heavy or whipping cream
1 can (15½-ounces) salmon, drained and flaked
1 cup mayonnaise
4 teaspoons prepared horseradish
2 teaspoons fresh dill, chopped, or ¾ teaspoon
dillweed
1 teaspoon lemon juice
½ teaspoon salt
½ teaspoon paprika
1 pimento-stuffed olive
About 5 radishes
About 3 celery stalks
Dill sprigs for garnish

About 4 hours before serving or day ahead: In 1-quart saucepan, sprinkle gelatin evenly over water. Cook over medium heat, stirring frequently, until gelatin is completely dissolved. Cover and refrigerate until mixture mounds slightly, about 30 minutes.

In small bowl with mixer at medium speed, beat heavy or whipping cream until stiff peaks form. In large bowl with mixer at medium speed, beat salmon, next 6 ingredients, and gelatin mixture until blended and smooth, scraping bowl often with rubber spatula. Fold whipped cream into salmon mixture. With pastry brush, lightly brush 6-cup fish or other favorite mold with salad oil. Spoon salmon mixture into mold; cover and refrigerate until set, about 3 hours.

To serve: Unmold fish mousse onto large platter. Cut olive crosswise in half. Thinly slice radishes and celery. Decorate head of fish with olive halves for eyes. Carefully place radish slices, overlapping slightly, in a row down center of fish. Press celery slices, about ⅛ inch deep, into mousse in a row on either side of radish row. Garnish platter with dill sprigs. Serves eight.

COLD SALMON
WITH GREEN SAUCE

2 cans (7¾ ounces each) salmon, flaked
4 onions, chopped
4 stuffed olives, chopped
2 hard-cooked eggs, sliced
½ cucumber, seeded and chopped
2 radishes, chopped
Salt and pepper to taste
½ dill pickle, chopped
1 cup mayonnaise
2 teaspoons minced parsley
2 teaspoons minced dill
4 spinach leaves, ground or blended to a paste
2 tablespoons sour cream
½ head Boston lettuce
1 lemon, quartered
Parsley sprigs for garnish

Combine salmon, onions, olives, eggs, cucumber, radishes, salt and pepper and pickle. To mayonnaise, beat in parsley, dill, spinach, and sour cream. Season to taste and pour over salmon. Arrange in a lettuce-lined bowl, garnish with lemon and parsley. Chill. Serves six.

139

COLD SALMON BISQUE

1 can (15½ ounces) salmon
1 small onion chopped
½ cup green pepper, chopped
½ clove garlic, minced
1 tablespoon butter
2 cups light cream
¼ cup chopped fresh dill
¼ teaspoon Worcestershire sauce
¼ teaspoon salt
⅛ teaspoon pepper
2 tablespoons dry sherry
1 tablespoon lemon juice

Drain salmon. Remove skin and large bones. Saute onion, green pepper, and garlic in butter until golden. Combine all ingredients except sherry and lemon juice and blend in blender for 1 minute at high speed. It should be very smooth. Refrigerate and chill at least 4 hours. Stir in sherry and lemon juice when just ready to serve. Serve in small bowls with lemon wedges. Serves four.

SALMON SPREAD

1 pound dry cottage cheese
1 can salmon
2 scallions (white part only) or ½ onion, cut into chunks
Dash Tabasco
Dash paprika
¼ cup pimento

Drain salmon thoroughly; remove all bones and skin. Place all ingredients in a blender or food processor and blend until smooth. For sandwiches, serve on rye bread or whole-wheat bagels with a slice of onion or tomato. Makes 1½ pints.

DEVILED SALMON-SALAD PLATTER

1 can (7¾ ounces) salmon, drained
Lettuce leaves
4 hard-cooked eggs, halved
1 small cucumber, sliced thin
1 medium tomato, cut in wedges
½ cup mayonnaise
2 teaspoons dry mustard
1 teaspoon dillweed

Invert salmon directly from can into center of large lettuce-lined platter. Surround with egg halves, cucumber and tomato. In small bowl mix mayonnaise, mustard and dillweed until smooth. Serve with salad. Serves four.

LOMI LOMI SALMON

1 can (15½ ounces) salmon
3 tomatoes diced
1/3 cup sliced green onions
½ cup finely chopped onion
2 tablespoons water
1 cup crushed ice

Shred salmon. Combine salmon, tomatoes, green onions, onion and water. Mix well. Chill at least several hours. Add ice just before serving.

SPICED SALMON

2 cups canned or cooked salmon, drained and flaked

Mix in a small pan:
1 cup mild vinegar
1 teaspoon whole cloves
½ teaspoon allspice berries
8 peppercorns
¼ teaspoon salt

Bring to the boiling point. Pour over the fish. Cover and let stand 2 hours. Drain and separate into flakes. Serves four.

TOMATO-SALMON RELISH

1 can (7¾ ounces) salmon, drained
6 medium-sized tomatoes (3 pounds)
4 green onions, sliced
1 can jalapeno peppers, finely chopped
¼ cup vinegar
1 teaspoon sugar
1 teaspoon salt

Dice tomatoes and place them in a large bowl. Add green onions, jalapeno peppers, vinegar, sugar, salt and salmon. Stir gently to blend. Cover and refrigerate at least 4 hours.

CREAMY SALMON PATE

1 can (7¾ ounces) salmon
1 package (8 ounces) cream cheese, at room temperature
1 package (.6 ounces) Green Goddess-flavored buttermilk salad dressing mix
1 tablespoon instant minced onion
1½ tablespoons lemon juice
1 teaspoon Worcestershire sauce
1 large clove garlic, minced or pressed
¼ teaspoon dry mustard
¼ cup finely chopped parsley

Line a small bowl (about 3-cup size) with clear plastic wrap; set aside. Drain the salmon and remove any bones or skin; set aside.

In a small bowl, beat together the cream cheese, dressing mix, onion, lemon juice, Worcestershire, garlic, and mustard until well blended. Stir in the parsley and the salmon. Spoon the mixture into the prepared bowl, pressing down firmly; smooth top. Cover and chill overnight or as long as 4 days.

To serve, invert bowl on a platter and unmold; peel off plastic wrap. Spread on crackers or fresh vegetables. Makes about 8 to 10 appetizer servings.

SALMON CUCUMBER PATE

Cucumber layer:
1 package (8 ounces) cream cheese
½ cup dairy cream
1 teaspoon salt
6 to 8 drops liquid red pepper seasoning
1 medium-size cucumber, pared, seeded and shredded
1 small onion, finely chopped
2 tablespoons snipped fresh dill

Salmon layer:
1 can (15½ ounces) salmon, drained, skin and bones removed
¾ cup mayonnaise
¼ cup finely chopped onion
2 tablespoons lemon juice
2 tablespoons prepared horseradish
2 tablespoons chopped parsley
1 teaspoon salt
1 teaspoon paprika
2 envelopes unflavored gelatin
½ cup cold water
1 cup heavy cream, whipped

Salmon caviar (about 2 tablespoons)
Cucumber slices
Lemon slices
Dill sprigs
Party rye bread and crackers

Cucumber layer:
   Beat cream cheese in medium-size bowl until softened and smooth: beat in sour cream, salt and red pepper seasoning. Stir in cucumber and onion. Set aside.

(continued)

144

Salmon layer:
Flake or mash salmon with a fork in a large bowl. Combine with mayonnaise, onion, lemon juice, horseradish, parsley, salt and paprika. Set aside.

Sprinkle gelatin over cold water in 1 cup measure; let soften 5 minutes. Set cup in simmering water; stir to dissolve gelatin. Remove from heat.

Stir 3 tablespoons gelatin liquid into cucumber mixture. Pour into 9-inch by 5-inch by 3-inch loaf pan, or 7- or 8-cup mold, rinsed with cold water. Chill while finishing salmon.

Stir remaining gelatin liquid into salmon mixture. Fold in whipped cream. Carefully spoon over cucumber layer in pan; cover. Chill 6 hours or overnight.

To serve, run tip of thin-bladed knife around top edge of mold. Dip mold quickly in and out of hot water. Cover with a chilled serving platter; invert; shake gently to release; lift off pan. Garnish with caviar, cucumber slices, lemon slices and dill. Serve with party rye bread and crackers.

SALMON CAPER

8 ounces cream cheese
½ teaspoon anchovy paste
1 can (7¾ ounces) salmon, drained and flaked
2 teaspoons chopped capers
1 tablespoon minced onion
Raw vegetables or crackers

Beat together cream cheese, anchovy paste, salmon, capers, and onion. Spread on crackers or use as dip for raw vegetables. Makes about 1¼ cups.

SALMON PARTY BALL

1 can (15½ ounces) salmon
1 package (8 ounces) cream cheese, softened
1 tablespoon lemon juice
1 teaspoon horseradish
2 teaspoon grated onion
¼ teaspoon salt
¼ teaspoon liquid smoke
¼ cup chopped pecans
3 teaspoons minced parsley

Clean salmon and flake into bowl. Add cream cheese, lemon juice, horseradish, onion, salt and liquid smoke. Mix well. Chill all day or overnight. Spread parsley and pecans on waxed paper. Roll salmon into a ball then roll over nuts and parsley to cover. Chill until served.

DILLED SALMON BUTTER

1 can (15½ ounces) salmon, well drained
½ cup (1 stick) unsalted butter, softened
1/3 cup fresh dill, finely chopped
¼ cup onion, chopped
½ teaspoon liquid red pepper seasoning
½ teaspoon salt
¼ teaspoon pepper

Combine salmon, butter, dill, onion, red pepper seasoning, salt and pepper in blender or food processor. Cover; whirl until well blended. Cover; refrigerate several hours or overnight. Makes 2 cups.

SUPER SALMON SPREAD

2 envelopes unflavored gelatin
¾ cup white cooking wine
1 cup boiling water
1 pint (16 ounces) sour cream
½ cup chili sauce
1 can (15½ ounces) salmon, drained and flaked

In a large bowl, sprinkle unflavored gelatin over wine; let stand 1 minute. Add boiling water and stir until gelatin is completely dissolved. With wire whisk or rotary beater, blend in sour cream and chili sauce. Stir in salmon. Turn into 6-cup mold or bowl; chill until firm. Makes about 5¼ cups spread.

SALMON SPREAD

1 package (3 ounces) cream cheese, softened
2 tablespoons grated onion
1 tablespoon lemon juice
1 teaspoon prepared white horseradish
½ teaspoon salt
¼ teaspoon pepper
1 can (15½ ounces) salmon, skin and bones discarded
1 green onion, sliced (for garnish)

Mix cream cheese, onion, lemon juice, horseradish, salt and pepper in medium-size bowl until blended. Finely flake salmon; add to mixture and stir until smooth and creamy. Spoon into crock or serving bowl; garnish with green onion. Chill until ready to serve. Makes 2 cups.

YANKEE SEASHELL SALAD

1 can (15½ ounces) salmon
4 cups cooked large shell macaroni
1 cup celery, sliced
½ cup carrots, diced
½ cup cooked peas
½ cup parsley, chopped
¼ cup green onion, chopped
½ cup vegetable oil
5 tablespoons lemon juice
2 tablespoons distilled white vinegar
1 teaspoon dill weed, crumbled
1 teaspoon celery seed
½ teaspoon salt
Crisp salad greens

Drain salmon. Combine macaroni, celery, carrots, peas, parsley and green onions. Combine oil, lemon juice, vinegar, dill weed, celery seed and salt in a screw-top jar. Shake well. Pour over macaroni mixture. Toss well. Refrigerate one-half hour. Toss again. Break salmon into large pieces; fold into macaroni mixture. Spoon salad into salad bowl lined with salad greens. Serves six.

SALMON SUPREME SPREAD

1 8-ounce package cream cheese
1 4-ounce package shredded cheddar cheese (1 cup)
1 can (7¾ ounces) salmon, drained, boned, finely flaked
½ teaspoon dried dillweed
¼ cup bottled onion salad dressing
Snipped parsley
Assorted crackers

Have cream cheese and cheddar cheese at room temperature. In small mixer bowl combine the cheeses, salmon, and dillweed. Gradually add the onion dressing, beating until fluffy. Cover and chill thoroughly. May be stored up to 4 or 5 days.

Shape salmon mixture into a log or ball; roll in snipped fresh parsley. Serve with assorted crackers. Makes about 2½ cups spread.

SALMON SALAD

1 cup Romaine lettuce leaves, torn
¼ cup canned salmon, drained and flaked
4 trimmed asparagus spears
½ cup cucumber, thin-sliced and unpeeled
1 tablespoon low-calorie herb dressing

Line salad plate with torn Romaine lettuce leaves. Top with salmon, asparagus spears and cucumber. Drizzle herb dressing over all. Serves one.

SALMON-PASTA SALAD

1 pound pasta (small shells or twists), cooked, drained and cooled
1 can salmon, drained (reserve liquid)
1 medium cucumber, peeled, seeded and diced
1 cup green peas, cooked and drained
¾ cup mayonnaise
1 tablespoon lemon juice
1 tablespoon prepared white horseradish
1 teaspoon prepared mustard
¼ teaspoon salt
Spinach leaves (optional)

Combine the pasta, salmon, cucumber, and peas. Mix the mayonnaise together with 1 tablespoon liquid from salmon and the remaining ingredients, except the spinach. Pour over pasta mixture and toss gently to blend. Chill. Serve on a bed of spinach, if desired. Serves six.

SALMON SALAD

1 can (7¾ ounces) salmon, flaked
2 scallions, chopped
½ stalk celery, diced
3 tablespoons Roquefort dressing

Remove bone and skin of salmon. Break in chunks in bowl. Mix scallions and celery with salmon. Turn into salad bowl and pour dressing over. This can also be served on lettuce leaves. Serves two.

WHITE BEAN AND SALMON SALAD

1 can (20 ounces) white kidney beans, rinsed and drained
2 tablespoons lemon juice
2 tablespoons parsley, minced
¼ teaspoon pepper
6 large lettuce leaves
1 can (7 ¾ ounces) salmon, drained (reserve 2 tablespoons liquid)
1 medium onion, sliced thin
2 tablespoons oil
8 ripe olives (for garnish)

Mix well the beans, lemon juice, parsley, and pepper. Line a large shallow bowl with the lettuce. Layer the bean mixture, salmon, and onion on the lettuce. Beat together the reserved salmon liquid and oil. Pour over the salad and garnish with the olives. Chill. Serves four.

COLD SALMON SALAD

1 can (7¾ ounces) salmon, flaked
½ cup cucumbers, chopped and peeled
½ cup mayonnaise
1 tablespoon capers
1 teaspoon chopped fresh or dried dill
1 squeeze lemon juice
½ teaspoon salt or to taste

Mix all ingredients and serve. Serves two.

SALMON-STUFFED TOMATO SALAD

1 tablespoon lemon juice
1 tart red apple, cored and diced
1 cup cooked peas
⅛ teaspoon salt
½ cup mayonnaise
1 can (7¾ ounces) salmon, drained, cleaned, and flaked
4 large tomatoes
Salad greens
1 hard-cooked egg, sliced (optional)

Sprinkle lemon juice over apples. Add peas, salt, and mayonnaise; toss to mix. Add salmon and toss gently. Chill at least one-half hour. Meanwhile, scald tomatoes in hot water and remove peel (if desired). Chill until ready to serve. To serve, remove stem ends from tomatoes, then cut from opposite stemmed end almost through bottom into six to eight sections. Spread open in petal fashion on salad greens. Fill with salmon mixture. Garnish with egg slices, if desired. Serves four.

49TH STATE SALAD

1 cup celery, diced
¼ cup onion, chopped
1 can (7¾ ounces) salmon
1½ cup carrots, shredded
½ cup salad dressing
1 small can shoestring potatoes or potato chips

Toss together. Just before serving, add shoestring potatoes or potato chips. Serves two.

BAKED SALMON SALAD

2 cans (15½ ounces each) salmon
2 cups thinly sliced celery
1 cup green pepper, chopped
½ cup onion, chopped
½ cup mayonnaise or salad dressing
1 tablespoon lemon juice
2 tablespoons Worcestershire sauce
½ teaspoon salt
Dash pepper
1 cup potato chips, coarsely crushed
Paprika

Drain and break salmon into large pieces. Combine all ingredients except potato chips and paprika. Place salad in 6 well-greased individual casseroles or 6-ounce custard cups. Sprinkle with potato chips and paprika. Place casseroles on a baking pan. Bake in a hot oven, 400°, for 15 to 20 minutes or until brown. Serves six.

GREEN GODDESS SALMON SALAD

1 can (15½ ounces) salmon
½ cup peeled, diced cucumber
½ cup diced green bell pepper
2 avocados, halved, seeded, peeled
Crisp salad greens
Bottled Green Goddess Dressing
Tomato, black olives and lemon wedges for garnish

Drain salmon. Combine salmon, cucumber and green pepper. Arrange avocado halves on 4 salad plates lined with salad greens. Spoon salmon mixture over and along side of each avocado. Garnish plates with tomato wedges, black olives and lemon wedges. Serve with dressing. Serves four.

LAYERED SALMON AND VEGETABLE SALAD

1 small head (1 to 1¼ pounds) cauliflower
1 to 1¼ pounds broccoli
1 can (15½ ounces) salmon
4 cups shredded iceberg lettuce
1 package (10 ounces) frozen peas
1½ cups mayonnaise
1½ teaspoons curry powder
¾ cup salted peanuts

Break cauliflower into flowerets; cut through stems into ¼-inch thick slices. Peel broccoli stems and slice ¼ inch thick; cut large flowers in halves or thirds.

Arrange cauliflower and sliced broccoli stems on a steamer rack. Cover and steam over rapidly boiling water until tender when pierced, about 5 minutes; add broccoli flowers the last 1 or 2 minutes. Let cool.

Drain salmon and break into chunks, discarding skin and bones. Place lettuce in a 3to 4-quart glass serving bowl. Top with cauliflower and broccoli the salmon and frozen peas. Blend mayonnaise and curry; spread evenly over top. Cover and chill 4 to 24 hours. Sprinkle with peanuts. Serves six to eight.

CURRY SALMON SALAD

1½ cups uncooked medium-size shell macaroni
Curry dressing (recipe follows)
½ cup each salted shelled sunflower seeds, finely chopped green pepper, and green onions (including tops)
1 cup chopped celery
1 package (10 ounces) frozen peas, thawed and well drained
1 can (7¾ ounces) salmon, skin and bone removed, drained
Parsley sprigs
3 hard-cooked eggs, thinly sliced

Cook the macaroni according to package directions; rinse and drain.

Prepare curry dressing as directed. In a large bowl, combine sunflower seeds, green pepper, green onions, celery, peas, and macaroni; pour dressing over and stir until blended; cover and chill 3 hours or overnight.

To serve, spoon the macaroni mixture onto a large serving platter; flake salmon into the center and garnish with parsley sprigs and egg slices. Serves six to eight.

Curry dressing:

In a small bowl, stir together ¾ cup mayonnaise, 1 ½ tablespoons each curry powder and prepared mustard, ¼ cup lemon juice, and 5 cloves garlic (minced or pressed) until well blended, then stir in 2 cups (about ½ pound) shredded sharp Cheddar cheese.

PICKLED SALMON
AND CAULIFLOWER SALAD

1 can (7¾ ounces) salmon, drained
1/3 cup vinegar
2 tablespoons water
¼ cup onion, chopped
½ teaspoon sugar
⅛ teaspoon pepper
1 bay leaf, broken in half
1 cup (about 5 ounces) blanched cauliflowerets
Spinach leaves
Minced parsley
Tomato wedges

Blanch cauliflower three minutes in boiling water; drain and cool.

Break into chunks. Combine vinegar, water, onion, sugar, pepper and bay leaf in saucepan. Bring to boil; simmer five minutes. Pour over salmon and cauliflower: marinate one-half to one hour, turning occasionally. Discard bay leaf.

Spoon salmon, cauliflower and marinade onto spinach-lined platter; sprinkle with parsley. Garnish with tomato wedges. Serves four.

SALMON-STUFFED EGGS

10 hard-cooked eggs
½ cup salmon, cooked or canned, drained and boned
1 anchovy fillet
½ cup butter or margarine
1 teaspoon Worcestershire sauce
Salt and pepper

Cut eggs into halves lengthwise. Take out yolks. Rub salmon, anchovy, and egg yolks through a sieve, or whirl in a blender. Cream butter. Add salmon mixture, Worcestershire, and seasonings to taste. Mix well. Stuff whites with mixture. Makes 20.

SALMON SALAD

1 10-ounce package frozen peas
1 10-ounce package frozen rice
4 ounces Swiss cheese, cubed
¼ teaspoon dried dillweed
1 can (7¾ ounces) salmon, drained, skin and bones removed, broken into chunks
2 cups spinach leaves
½ cup shredded carrot
½ cup creamy cucumber salad dressing

Place peas in a colander under cold running water for 2 minutes to thaw. Place rice pouch under warm running water until mixture can be broken up, about 5 minutes. Toss together rice, peas, cheese, and dillweed. Add salmon; toss lightly. Line 4 plates with spinach; place salmon mixture on top. Arrange carrot around edge. Pass dressing. Serves four.

SALMON PLATTER

½ pound uncooked asparagus
¼ cup Italian salad dressing
Leaf lettuce
1 can (15½ ounces) salmon, drained
6 medium tomatoes
1 large cucumber, thinly sliced
Carrot sticks
1 carton (8 ounces) unflavored yogurt
½ cup mayonnaise or salad dressing
1 tablespoon snipped chives
½ teaspoon garlic salt

Break off tough ends of asparagus at point where stalks snap easily. Cut diagonally into very thin slices; toss with salad dressing. Cover and refrigerate 1 hour.

Arrange lettuce on large platter. Break salmon into chunks, removing skin and bones; mound salmon on lettuce in center of platter. Cut each tomato into a flower. Drain asparagus, spoon into tomato flowers. Arrange tomatoes, cucumber and carrot sticks around salmon.

Mix yogurt, mayonnaise, chives and garlic salt; spoon 2 tablespoons onto salmon. Serve remaining dressing with salad. Serves six.

SUMMER SALMON

1½ cups mayonnaise
¼ cup milk
1 tablespoon onion, chopped
½ teaspoon dillweed
2 cups shredded lettuce
2 cups (7 ounces) shell macaroni, cooked, drained
½ cup pitted ripe olive halves
2 cups chopped tomato
2 cups cucumber slices, halved
1 can (15½ ounces) salmon, drained, flaked

Combine mayonnaise, milk, onion and dill; mix well. Chill.

In 3-quart bowl, layer lettuce, combine macaroni and olives, tomato, cucumber and salmon; top with ¾ cup dressing. Garnish with dillweed, if desired. Serve with remaining dressing. Serves six.

SALMON AND AVOCADO

3 avocados
1 package (3 ounces) cream cheese, softened
1 can (15½ ounces) salmon
2 teaspoons Worcestershire sauce
1½ teaspoons salt
⅛ teaspoon pepper
1 tablespoon lemon juice

Beat cream cheese, salmon, Worcestershire, salt and pepper until fluffy. Cut avocados in half, remove pits, and brush with lemon juice. Fill each avocado with cheese and salmon mixture. Chill. Serves six.

OPEN-FACED
SALMON-SALAD CROISSANTS

4 croissants, split lengthwise
1 can (15½ ounces) salmon, drained, broken in chunks
3 tablespoons plain yogurt or sour cream
3 tablespoons lemon juice, or to taste
1½ tablespoons snipped fresh dill or 1½ teaspoons dried
1 medium-size cucumber, scored with fork if desired, sliced thin
Dill sprigs for garnish (optional)

Heat croissants in preheated 325° oven 10 minutes until crisp; cool. Gently toss salmon, yogurt, lemon juice and snipped dill until well mixed. For each serving, place a croissant cut-sides up on plate. Spoon salmon mixture over each half. Top with cucumber slices and dill sprigs. Serves four.

SALMON-AVOCADO CANAPES

Crackers
1 can (15½ ounces) salmon
1 avocado
1 tablespoon olive or salad oil
1 clove garlic, finely chopped
1½ teaspoons onion, grated
½ teaspoon salt
4 drops Tabasco

Drain and flake salmon. Peel avocado, remove seed, mash. Combine all ingredients. Toss lightly. Serve on crackers. Makes about 1 pint of spread.

CUCUMBER BOATS
WITH SALMON SALAD

2 large cucumbers, peeled, halved lengthwise
and seeded to form boats
2 medium cucumbers, peeled, seeded, and diced
fine
1 medium carrot, shredded
1 rib celery, chopped coarse
3 medium scallions, with tops, minced
½ cup mayonnaise
2 teaspoons lemon juice
1 teaspoon prepared mustard
¼ teaspoon salt
⅛ teaspoon pepper
1 can salmon, drained
Watercress

Dry the cucumber boats with paper towel, then chill. In a bowl, mix well the diced cucumbers, carrot, celery, scallions, mayonnaise, lemon juice, mustard, salt and pepper. Gently stir in the salmon, breaking it up as little as possible. Cover and chill about 1 hour, or until cold. To serve, fill each cucumber boat with about ½ cup salad. Garnish with watercress, and serve on a bed of watercress. Serves four.

Note: Best served soon after preparation to prevent the cucumbers from making the salad watery.

TROPICAL SALMONBURGERS

6 sandwich buns, split, toasted
1 can (15½ ounces) salmon, flaked
¼ cup lemon juice
3 tablespoons pickle relish
1 teaspoon salt
6 slices canned pineapple
1/3 cup grated process cheese

   Combine flaked salmon, lemon juice, pickled relish, and salt. Arrange pineapple slices on greased baking sheet. Place 1/3 cup salmon mixture on each pineapple slice. Sprinkle about 1 tablespoon cheese over each salmonburger. Bake in a 400° oven for 5 minutes, or until cheese melts. Place a salmonburger between halves of toasted sandwich buns. Serve while hot. Makes six sandwiches.

SALMON AND AVOCADO SANDWICHES

1/3 cup mayonnaise
2 teaspoons lime juice, divided
1 green onion, sliced
1 tablespoon fresh minced dill or 1 teaspoon dillweed
1 can (15½ ounces) salmon, drained, divided in chunks
2 small avocados, sliced
8 slices whole-wheat bread, each spread with 1 teaspoon margarine and toasted
4 lettuce leaves

In medium bowl, stir mayonnaise, 1 teaspoon lime juice, the green onion and dill until blended; gently stir in salmon; set aside. Sprinkle avocado with remaining 1 teaspoon lime juice; set aside. Layer each of 4 slices toast with a lettuce leaf, ¼ salmon mixture and avocado slices. Top with remaining toast. Serves four.

SALMON BOATS

1 can (7¾ ounces) salmon, drained, flaked
1 tablespoon onion, chopped
2 teaspoons chives, chopped
1 hard-cooked egg
2 avocados, halved and pitted
Dill Sauce

Combine salmon, onion, chives and chopped egg white. Place avocados on individual lettuce-covered plates. Fill with salmon mixture. Top with Dill Sauce; garnish with sieved egg yolk. Serves four.

Dill Sauce:
½ cup mayonnaise
¼ teaspoon dillweed

Combine ingredients; mix well.

163

SALMON-TOMATO APPETIZER

Pastry for one-crust 9-inch pie
½ cup long grain rice
1 cup water
1/3 cup creamy cucumber salad dressing
1 envelope unflavored gelatin
1½ cups vegetable juice cocktail
2 tablespoons lemon juice
½ teaspoon sugar
¼ teaspoon celery salt
1 can (15½ ounces) salmon, drained, boned, and flaked
¼ cup green onion, chopped
¼ cup celery, finely chopped
3 tablespoons creamy cucumber salad dressing
Celery leaves (optional)
Pitted ripe olives (optional)

Prepare pastry. Line a 10-inch flan pan or pie plate with the pastry. Prick sides and bottom. Bake in a 450° oven for 10 to 12 minutes or until golden. Cool on a wire rack. Cook rice in water, covered, for 15 minutes or until tender. Combine hot cooked rice with the 1/3 cup dressing; press into pastry shell. Chill. In small saucepan soften the gelatin in ¾ cup of the vegetable juice cocktail. Heat over low heat, stirring constantly, until gelatin is dissolved. Remove from heat. Stir in the remaining vegetable juice cocktail, 1 tablespoon of the lemon juice, the sugar, and celery salt. Chill until mixture is partially set (consistency of unbeaten egg whites).

For filling, combine the salmon, green onion, chopped celery, the 3 tablespoons salad dressing, and the remaining lemon juice. To assemble, top rice mixture with the salmon mixture, pressing lightly. Spoon partially set tomato mixture atop. Chill tart until firm. To serve, garnish with celery leaves and pitted ripe olives; cut into thin wedges. Makes 12 appetizer servings.

SALMON RING WITH PEAS

2 eggs, lightly beaten
1 can cream of mushroom soup
4 saltines, crushed
¼ cup green pepper
1 tablespoon parsley, minced
1 tablespoon lemon juice
1 teaspoon onion, grated
Pepper
Celery salt
1 can (15½ ounces) salmon, drained and flaked
1 package frozen peas

Combine the eggs, half the soup, crumbs, green pepper, parsley, lemon juice, onion, dash of pepper, and a good pinch of celery salt. Stir into the salmon and spoon into a ring mold. Bake 40 to 50 minutes in a 350° oven and unmold onto a hot plate. Cook the peas in ½ cup boiling salted water, letting them simmer 2 minutes after the water comes to a boil again. Drain and mix gently with the rest of the mushroom soup which has been heated just to the boiling point. If it seems too thick, add a little skim milk. Pour the pea mixture into the center of the salmon ring. Serves four to six.

JELLIED SALMON RINGS

1 envelope unflavored gelatin
¼ cup cold soup stock or water
½ cup hot soup stock or water
2 cups flaked salmon, cooked or canned
1 tablespoon minced parsley
1 medium onion, chopped fine
½ teaspoon salt
¼ teaspoon paprika
1 tablespoon lemon juice
3 tablespoons low-fat cottage cheese
1 bunch watercress

Soften gelatin in cold liquid. Add hot liquid and stir until gelatin is dissolved. Chill until the consistency of unbeaten egg white. Mix salmon, parsley, onion, and seasoning. Blend lemon juice into cottage cheese and add to salmon mixture. Combine with gelatin mixture and pour into 6 individual ring molds and chill until firm. Unmold on beds of watercress. Serves six.

MOLDED SALMON

1 tablespoon unflavored gelatin
1/3 cup cold water
2 egg yolks, slightly beaten
1 teaspoon salt
1 teaspoon dry mustard
1½ tablespoons melted butter or margarine
¾ cup milk
2 tablespoons vinegar
1 can (15½ ounces) salmon, drained and flaked
½ cup sliced olives

Soften gelatin in water. Combine egg yolks, seasonings and butter in top of double boiler. Stir in milk gradually. Cook over hot water for 5 to 6 minutes or until thickened, stirring constantly. Add gelatin and stir until dissolved. Add vinegar, salmon, and olives. Pour into a 1-quart mold. Chill until firm. Serve on a bed of lettuce. Serves six.

PASTRY-WRAPPED SALMON RING

1 can (15½ ounces) salmon
1½ cups soft bread crumbs (2 slices)
2 eggs, beaten
½ cup celery, finely chopped
2 tablespoons green pepper, finely chopped
2 tablespoons onion, finely chopped
1 tablespoon lemon juice
1 8-ounce package (8) refrigerated crescent rolls
Sour cream (optional)
Snipped chives (optional)
Tomato wedges (optional)
Celery leaves (optional)

Generously grease a 5-cup ovenproof ring mold; set aside. In a mixing bowl, drain and flake salmon, removing and discarding skin and bones. Add the bread crumbs, eggs, celery, green pepper, onion and lemon juice. Separate crescent rolls into triangles. Arrange triangles in ring mold, alternating points and wide ends of triangles so dough drapes over center and outer edges of mold. Pat the dough lightly to line the mold. Pack the salmon mixture into the dough-lined mold. Turn the ends of dough over the salmon to cover. Press to seal. Bake in a 375° oven for 30 minutes. Loosen edges. Invert onto serving platter. Serve with sour cream and chives. Garnish platter with tomato wedges and celery leaves. Serves four to six.

SALMON SOUR CREAM MOLD

1 envelope unflavored gelatin
½ cup cold water
1 envelope sour cream sauce mix
½ cup mayonnaise or salad dressing
2 teaspoons lemon juice
¼ teaspoon dried dillweed
1 can (15½ ounces) salmon
½ cup celery, diced

Soften gelatin in cold water; stir over boiling water until gelatin dissolves. Cool. Prepare sour cream sauce mix according to package directions. Blend in mayonnaise, lemon juice, and dillweed; gradually stir in gelatin. Drain salmon, discarding skin and large bones; flake. Fold salmon and celery into sour cream mixture; turn into 3-cup mold. Chill until set, 4 to 5 hours. Unmold; garnish with carrot curls. Serves four.

SALMON QUICHE

1 package (11 ounces) pie crust mix or sticks
1 can (15½ ounces) salmon, drained and flaked
4 green onions, chopped (about 6 tablespoons)
8 eggs
4 cups whipping cream or light cream
1½ teaspoons salt
½ teaspoon sugar
¼ teaspoon cayenne red pepper

Prepare pastry for two One-Crust Pies as directed on package. Divide salmon and onions between pastry-lined pie plates.

Beat eggs slightly; beat in whipping cream, salt, sugar and red pepper.

Heat oven to 425°. Pour half of the egg mixture on salmon and onions in each pie plate. Bake 15 minutes. Reduce oven temperature to 300° and bake until knife inserted 1 inch from edge comes out clean, about 45 minutes. Let stand 10 minutes before cutting. Serves twelve.

SALMON-SHRIMP MOLD

2 envelopes unflavored gelatin
1 cup cold water
1 cup boiling water
¼ cup lemon juice
1 teaspoon salt
⅛ teaspoon hot-pepper sauce
1 cup mayonnaise
8 ounces cleaned, cooked shrimps
1 can (15½ ounces) salmon, drained, bones and
skin removed, flaked
½ cup celery, finely chopped
¼ cup each green onions and pimento, finely
chopped
Celery leaves and pimento strips for garnish
(optional)

   In large bowl, sprinkle gelatin over cold water; let
stand 3 minutes to soften. Add boiling water; stir
until gelatin completely dissolves. Stir in lemon juice,
salt, pepper sauce and mayonnaise until well blended.
Set aside half the shrimps for garnish (select the most
attractive); chop the rest. Stir salmon, chopped
shrimps, celery, green onions and pimento into gelatin
mixture until blended. Turn into 6-cup mold; chill at
least 4 hours or until firm. Unmold; garnish with
reserved shrimps, celery leaves and pimento strips.
Serves twelve.

SALMON AND VEGETABLE PIE

1 pint Garden Medley or Italian-Style vegetables
Pastry for 2-crust 9-inch pie
½ cup sour cream
1 tablespoon all-purpose flour
1 tablespoon finely snipped fresh dill or 1 teaspoon dried dillweed
1 tablespoon snipped parsley
2 teaspoons Worcestershire sauce
1 can (15½ salmon, drained, lightly flaked, skin
and bones removed
1½ cups (6 ounces) shredded sharp American
cheese
Milk
Yellow cornmeal (optional)

Cook the canned or frozen vegetable mix according
to recipe directions. On lightly floured surface, roll
half the pastry to a 12-inch circle. Transfer to a 9-inch
pie plate; trim pastry even with rim. Set aside. Stir
together the sour cream, flour, dill, parsley, and Worcestershire; stir into heated vegetable mixture in
saucepan. Gently stir in salmon and cheese. Turn
into pastry shell.

For crust top, roll out the remaining pastry to a
10-inch circle. Cut a design in pastry or slits for
escape of steam; place atop filled pie plate. Trim top
crust to ½ inch beyond edge of pie plate. Fold extra
pastry under bottom crust; flute edge.

Brush top with milk. Sprinkle with cornmeal, if
desired. Bake in a 375° oven 45 to 55 minutes. If
necessary, cover edge with foil to prevent overbrown-
ing. Let stand 15 minutes before serving. Garnish
with additional fresh dill, if desired. Serves eight.

SALMON POT PIE

3 tablespoons onion, chopped
4 tablespoons butter or margarine
¼ cup flour
2 cups milk
¼ teaspoon salt
⅛ teaspoon pepper
1 can (15½ ounces) salmon, broken into chunks
1 cup diced cooked carrots
1 cup frozen peas
½ cup grated cheese
Biscuits for topping

Saute onion in melted butter until tender. Add flour and blend. Slowly add milk, stirring occasionally. Cook until thickened. Season with salt and pepper.

Add salmon chunks, carrots, uncooked peas, and grated cheese. Pour into casserole. Top with rolled biscuit dough.

Bake in hot oven (425°) 20 minutes, until biscuits are brown and mixture is bubbly. Serves four to six.

PATE AU SAUMON
(SALMON PIE)

2 medium potatoes, peeled and cubed
1 medium onion, chopped very fine
4 tablespoons butter
1 can (15½ ounces) salmon, cleaned of skin and bones
3 to 4 tablespoons hot milk
Salt and pepper
Top and bottom crusts for one pie

Cook potatoes and onion together until tender; drain and mash, adding butter and mixing until smooth. Combine salmon with the potato mixture; add hot milk, and salt and pepper to taste. Spoon onto bottom crust; add top crust and seal. Brush top crust with a little milk and sprinkle with paprika if desired. Bake at 400° for 10 minutes; reduce heat to 350° and bake 45 minutes longer. Serves four to six.

SALMON PIE

1 can (15½ ounces) salmon, flaked
1 tablespoon onion, grated
¼ pound process sharp cheese, thinly sliced
1 can condensed cream of celery soup
1 cup flour
1½ teaspoon baking powder
½ teaspoon salt
3 tablespoons shortening
1 egg
½ cup milk

Drain salmon, reserving liquid. Flake with fork, removing bones and skin. Place in bottom of 9-inch pie pan. Top with onion, 2 tablespoons salmon liquid and cheese. Spread 1/3 can celery soup over cheese.

To make crust, sift together flour, baking powder and salt. Cut in shortening until mixture resembles coarse crumbs. Combine egg and ¼ cup milk. Add to dry ingredients and mix only until all the flour is moistened.

Place on lightly floured board and knead 8 or 10 times. Roll out slightly larger than top of pie pan. Place over salmon mixture and flute edges against edge of pan. Cut a 1-inch square out of center of dough for steam vent.

Bake pie in moderate oven, 375° until lightly browned, 25 to 30 minutes. Cut in wedges. Serve topped with sauce made by heating remaining 2/3 can celery soup and ¼ cup milk. Serves six.

SALMON RABBIT PIE

1 can (15½ ounces) salmon, flaked
1 cup cooked peas, drained
2 tablespoons green pepper, finely chopped
1 cup grated cheese
½ cup milk
2 tablespoons mayonnaise
1/3 cup milk
1 cup Bisquick

Heat oven to 450°. Mix salmon, peas, green pepper: spread in greased 10 inch by 6 inch baking dish. Blend cheese, milk: pour over salmon. Mix mayonnaise, 1/3 cup milk and Bisquick with fork. Drop with spoon on salmon mixture. Bake 10 to 15 minutes until browned. Serves six.

SALMON CUSTARD PIE

Unbaked 9-inch pie shell
¼ cup green onion, chopped
2 tablespoons butter
1 can (15½ ounces) salmon
1 teaspoon dried dillweed
½ teaspoon salt
¼ teaspoon pepper
1 cup light cream, scalded
4 eggs, slightly beaten

Bake pie shell in moderate oven (375°) 5 minutes.
Cook onion in butter until soft. Drain salmon, reserving ¼ cup salmon liquid. Remove bones from salmon.
Place salmon, dill, salt, pepper and salmon liquid in bowl. Mash with fork until well mixed. Add green onion, cream and eggs. Mix well.
Pour into pie shell and bake in moderate oven (375°) until mixture is set, 35 to 40 minutes. Serves six.

SALMON PIE WITH BISCUITS

1 can (15½ ounces) salmon, drained and flaked
1 package (10 ounces) frozen peas, cooked
3 tablespoons butter or margarine
3 tablespoons enriched flour
¼ teaspoon salt
Dash ground black pepper
2 cups milk

Biscuits:
2 cups sifted enriched flour
1 tablespoon baking powder
½ teaspoon salt
¼ cup shortening
2/3 to ¾ cup milk

Combine salmon and peas.

Melt butter in saucepan. Stir in flour, salt, and pepper. Add milk gradually and cook until thickened, stirring constantly. Add salmon and peas and pour into 2-quart casserole.

Biscuits:

Sift together flour, baking powder, and salt. Cut or rub in shortening until mixture is crumbly. Add milk to make a soft dough. Turn out on lightly floured board or pastry cloth and knead gently 30 seconds. Roll out ½-inch thick. Cut with floured shamrock biscuit cutter or cut around shamrock pattern.

Arrange biscuits on top of salmon mixture. Place remaining biscuits on ungreased baking sheet. Bake casserole in a 425° oven 20 to 25 minutes. Bake remaining biscuits 12 to 15 minutes. Serves six.

SALMON CHEESE LOAF

1 can (15½ ounces) salmon, flaked
1½ cups cheese, grated
1 egg, well beaten
3 tablespoons milk
1 tablespoon melted butter
½ teaspoon salt
Dash pepper
Cracker or bread crumbs to make a stiff mixture

Combine all ingredients. Pack into a loaf pan. Cover the top with buttered crumbs. Bake at 375° until golden brown. Serves six.

SALMON LOAF
WITH CRAB SAUCE

1 can (15½ ounces) salmon, drained and flaked
2 slices bread, crumbed
¼ cup evaporated skim milk
1 egg
¼ cup chicken bouillon
¼ cup celery, finely chopped
½ teaspoon onion salt
Crab Sauce (recipe follows)

Mix all ingredients thoroughly. Pour into greased dish. Bake. Serve on warm platter with crab sauce poured over. Serves four.

Crab Sauce:
1 can (6 ounces) crabmeat, drained, flaked and cartilage removed
¼ cup chicken broth or clam juice
1 tablespoon lemon juice

Mix all ingredients well.

CURRIED SALMON-RICE LOAF

1 can (7¾ ounces) salmon
3 cups rice, cooked
1/3 cup scallions, chopped
2 teaspoons curry powder
3 teaspoons lemon juice
3 tablespoons cider vinegar
1 teaspoon garlic powder
Tomatoes, to garnish
Curry Sauce (recipe follows)

Flake the salmon, removing any skin and bones, and add the salmon with its liquid to the cooked rice. Add the scallions, curry, lemon juice, vinegar and garlic powder. Pack the mixture into a small loaf pan lined with plastic wrap. Refrigerate for several hours. When ready to serve, unmold the salmon and arrange it on lettuce leaves. Garnish with sliced fresh tomatoes, if desired. Serves four.

Curry Sauce:
3¼ cups chicken broth
3 tablespoons cornstarch
1 teaspoon curry powder
¼ teaspoon dry mustard
2 tablespoons undiluted frozen apple juice concentrate, thawed

Bring the chicken broth to a boil in a skillet. Dissolve the cornstarch in a bowl of water. Add this to the broth, stirring until thickened. Add the mustard and curry to the apple juice and stir.

SALMON-DILL LOAF

2 envelopes unflavored gelatin
1 can (15½ ounces) salmon, drained and flaked
2 (3-ounce) packages cream cheese, at room temperature
1 cup sour cream or plain yogurt
1 ½ tablespoons white prepared horseradish
2 teaspoons lemon juice
¼ teaspoon pepper
2 scallions, sliced thin
1 tablespoon snipped fresh dill or ½ teaspoon dried dill
½ cup heavy cream, whipped
Dill sprigs and tomato slices for garnish (optional)

Sprinkle gelatin over ½ cup cold water in a small saucepan. Stir over moderate heat until gelatin is completely dissolved and liquid is almost boiling. Remove from heat; stir in ¼ cup cold water. In a large bowl beat salmon, cream cheese, sour cream, horseradish, lemon juice and pepper with an electric mixer until well blended. Beat in dissolved gelatin. Stir in scallions and snipped dill. Gently but thoroughly fold in whipped cream. Pour salmon mixture into a lightly oiled 8½-inch by 4½-inch by 2½-inch loaf pan. Cover and refrigerate 2 hours, or until firm. Before serving, turn out loaf onto a platter. Garnish with dill sprigs and tomato slices. Cut into 16 slices.

SALMON CROQUETTES

¾ pound potatoes cut into small pieces
1 can (15½ ounces) salmon, drained and flaked
½ cup chopped green onion
1 egg, slightly beaten
1 tablespoon chopped parsley
½ teaspoon ground ginger
6 tablespoons all-purpose flour
Vegetable oil for frying

Cook potatoes in water until tender. Mash until smooth. Add salmon, green onion, egg, parsley and ginger. Stir to mix well. Shape into 8 equal-sized oval logs. Roll into flour to coat. Fry in hot vegetable oil until golden brown and crusty on all sides.

SALMON CROQUETTES

1 can (15½ ounces) salmon
¼ cup cracker crumbs
½ teaspoon onion, grated
½ teaspoon green pepper, grated
1 large well-beaten egg (or 2 small ones)
½ teaspoon salt
Cayenne pepper
1 tablespoon celery tops, chopped

Mince the fish; add salt, pepper, onion, green pepper and celery (or parsley if you prefer). Moisten with raw egg to proper consistency to make cone-shaped cakes. Dip them into another well-beaten egg, roll in bread crumbs (or cornmeal) with a bit of salt and black pepper added and deep fry until lightly brown. Serves four to six.

SALMON-CORN CAKES

3 eggs
2 tablespoons flour
2 teaspoons lemon juice
1 teaspoon salt
2 drops red pepper sauce
Dash of pepper
1 can (12 ounces) whole kernel corn, drained
1 can (7¾ ounces) salmon, drained and flaked
Pimento Sauce (recipe follows)

Grease heated griddle if necessary. Mix eggs, flour, lemon juice, salt, pepper sauce and pepper with hand beater until foamy. Stir in corn and salmon.

Drop mixture by generous ¼ cupfuls onto hot griddle; flatten slightly. Cook until golden brown, about 3 minutes on each side. Grease griddle as necessary. Serve corn cakes with Pimento Sauce. Serves four.

Pimento Sauce:
½ cup sour cream
¼ cup American cheese, grated
2 tablespoons pimento, chopped

Heat all ingredients just to boiling over low heat, stirring constantly.

SALMON PUFFS

1 can (15½ ounces) salmon
12 slices tomato
6 slices white bread, toasted
1 cup mayonnaise or salad dressing
Dash of cayenne
1 tablespoon parsley, chopped
2 tablespoons lemon juice
2 egg whites

Heat broiler. Drain salmon; remove bones and skin; flake. Place 2 slices of tomato on each piece of toast. Arrange a layer of salmon over the tomatoes. Combine mayonnaise or salad dressing, cayenne, parsley, and lemon juice. Beat egg whites until stiff but not dry. Fold mayonnaise mixture into egg whites. Spoon mixture over each sandwich. Broil until puffy and lightly browned. Serves six.

SALMON PUFFS

1 can (15½ ounces) salmon, drained and flaked
1½ cups soft bread crumbs (about 4 slices)
1 cup sour cream
2 eggs, separated
2 tablespoons onion, minced
¼ teaspoon salt
Dash pepper
Seasoned bread crumbs
Vegetable oil
Lemon wedges

Remove skin and bones from salmon. In large bowl, combine salmon, crumbs, sour cream, egg yolks, onions, salt and pepper. Mix well. Beat egg whites until stiff; fold into salmon mixture. On large sheet of wax paper, sprinkle seasoned bread crumbs. Drop heaping tablespoons of salmon mixture into crumbs, coating all sides. In large skillet, heat oil (enough to brown the puffs). Serve hot with lemon wedges. Serves six.

POTATO-SALMON PUFF

2 cups mashed potatoes (4 or 5 medium potatoes)
1 tablespoon unsalted butter or margarine
1 can (15½ ounces) salmon, undrained
1 cup sour cream
½ cup parsley, chopped
½ cup celery, chopped
1/3 cup onion, chopped
¼ cup red or green pepper, chopped
1 teaspoon salt, or to taste
¼ teaspoon freshly ground black pepper
4 eggs separated
Parsley, Tartar sauce (optional)

Wash potatoes and put in a large saucepan with boiling water to cover. Put on lid and simmer over medium heat for 40 minutes, or until tender. Peel potatoes and mash with a potato masher. Add butter.

In large mixing bowl, flake salmon with liquid. Add mashed potatoes, sour cream, parsley, celery, onion, red pepper, salt and pepper. Mix well. Slightly beat the egg yolks and add to salmon mixture. Beat egg whites until stiff and fold in. Turn into greased 2½-quart baking dish.

Bake in 350° oven for 1 hour, or until the tip of a knife inserted in center comes out clean. Garnish with parsley and serve with tartar sauce. Serves six to eight.

SALMON PHYLLO PUFFS

½ cup uncooked long-grain rice
½ pound mushrooms, thinly sliced
½ cup green onions, chopped
3 tablespoons butter
3 tablespoons lemon juice
1 can (15½ ounces) salmon, drained and flaked
3 hard-cooked eggs, chopped
1 teaspoon dillweed
1 package (1 pound) phyllo or strudel pastry
1 cup (2 sticks) butter or margarine, melted

Cook rice following package directions. Saute mushrooms and green onions in butter in a large skillet just until lightly browned. Add lemon juice and stir. Mix rice, salmon, eggs, dillweed and mushroom mixture in medium-size bowl.

Place phyllo pastry on clean work surface. Cut pastry into 4 equal lengthwise strips. Work with 2 stacks of strips at a time; cover other 2 stacks with plastic wrap. Brush 2 top strips with melted butter. Place a rounded teaspoon of filling at one end of both strips. Working with the top leaf, fold one corner to the opposite side, forming a triangle. Continue folding as you would a flag, keeping the triangle shape, to the other end of the strip. Repeat with the second strip, forming a second triangle puff. Repeat with the remaining melted butter, filling and pastry. Arrange triangles on ungreased 15-inch by 10-inch by 1-inch jelly roll pan.

Bake in preheated hot oven (425°) for 15 minutes or until golden brown. Serve hot. Makes about eight dozen puffs.

SALMON PATTIES
WITH TARTAR SAUCE

1 can (15½ ounces) salmon, drained and flaked
1 cup cold mashed potatoes
1 egg
1 medium-size onion, chopped fine (about ½ cup)
½ cup dry bread crumbs
¾ teaspoon salt
¼ teaspoon pepper
¼ cup vegetable oil
Tartar Sauce (recipe follows)

In medium-size bowl, mix salmon, potatoes, egg, onion, ¼ cup bread crumbs, salt and pepper. Shape mixture into 4 patties. Coat with remaining ¼ cup bread crumbs. Heat oil in large heavy skillet. Add patties and cook over medium heat, turning once, 10 minutes or until heated through and golden brown. Serve with Tartar Sauce. Serves four.

Tartar Sauce:
In small bowl, mix well ½ cup mayonnaise, 3 tablespoons sweet-pickle relish and 2 teaspoons prepared mustard. Makes ¾ cup.

DEEP DISH SALMON PIZZA

1 can (7¾ ounces) salmon
1 (8-ounce) package refrigerated crescent rolls
1/3 cup tomato sauce
½ teaspoon salt
⅛ teaspoon pepper
¼ teaspoon garlic powder
½ teaspoon oregano
¼ cup grated Parmesan cheese
1 green pepper, sliced
1 tomato, sliced
1 cup shredded Monterey Jack cheese

Drain salmon and flake. Press crescent roll dough on bottom and sides of 9-inch-square baking pan. Bake at 400° for 7 minutes. Remove from oven and spread with tomato sauce. Sprinkle with salt, pepper, garlic powder, oregano and Parmesan cheese. Top with salmon, green pepper and tomato. Sprinkle over Monterey Jack cheese. Bake at 425° for 15 minutes. Serves four.

SALMON CHEESECAKE

1 cup cracker crumbs
3 tablespoons butter or margarine, melted
2 packages (8 ounces) cream cheese
3 eggs
¾ cup sour cream
1 can (7¾ ounces) salmon, flaked
1 teaspoon lemon juice
½ teaspoon onion powder
⅛ teaspoon pepper

Combine crumbs and margarine; press into bottom of 9-inch Springform pan. Bake at 350° for 10 minutes.

Combine cream cheese, eggs and ¼ cup sour cream, mixing with electric mixer until blended. Add remaining ingredients and mix well. Pour over crust. Bake at 325° for 45 minutes. Loosen cake from rim of pan. Cool. Remove rim. Spread over remaining sour cream. Serves four to six.

SALMON CAKES

1 can (15½ ounces) salmon, flaked
2 ounces cracker meal
½ teaspoon nutmeg
2 teaspoons salt
½ teaspoon ground pepper
1 egg
12 ounces mashed potatoes
½ cup flour

Mix cracker meal, nutmeg, salt, ground pepper and salmon. Beat egg and add to cracker meal mixture, then mix in mashed potatoes and flour. Roll into patties and fry at 350° for 3 to 5 minutes until golden brown. The dish is better if the mix is refrigerated 4 to 6 hours before forming into patties. Serves four to six.

BAKED SALMON ROLLS

1 can (15½ ounces) salmon
¼ cup pimento
2 cloves garlic, minced fine
2 scallions, chopped
1 teaspoon Dijon mustard
1 teaspoon arrowroot powder or cornstarch
½ teaspoon celery salt
¼ teaspoon Tabasco (optional)
8 slices whole-wheat or sourdough bread

Place the salmon with all the other ingredients except the bread in a blender and blend until smooth. Remove the crust from the bread. Flatten each slice with a rolling pin or the side of a glass. Spread the salmon mixture generously on each slice of bread. Roll up the slices of bread and place on a non-stick baking sheet. Bake in a 350° oven for 20 minutes. Cut the rolls in half and serve warm. Any remaining salmon mixture may be used as a dip with vegetable chips. Makes 16 rolls.

SALMON PATTIES

1 can (15½ ounces) salmon, drained and flaked
4 eggs
2 tablespoons cream
1/3 to ½ cup bread crumbs
½ teaspoon salt
Pinch of pepper
2 tablespoons cold water
Bread crumbs for coating
Butter or margarine
2 cups medium white sauce
½ cup celery, finely cut

Combine salmon, 2 of the eggs slightly beaten, cream, bread crumbs, salt and pepper. Mix and shape into 12 flat cakes. Beat slightly remaining 2 eggs with water. Dip cakes into egg and coat lightly with crumbs. Saute in butter until well browned on both sides. Serve on hot toast with sauce to which celery is added. Serves four.

SEA BURGERS

1 can (7¾ ounces) salmon
½ pound sharp cheese, grated
1 cup celery, minced
¼ cup onion, chopped
¼ cup sweet relish
½ cup catsup
¼ cup salad dressing
½ teaspoon salt
Dash pepper

Combine ingredients well. Spread mixture on 12 buttered buns. Place on cookie sheet, cover with foil. Heat 20 minutes at 350°. Serve hot. Makes 12 sandwiches.

SALMONBURGERS

6 hamburger rolls
1 can (15½ ounces) salmon
½ cup onion, chopped
¼ cup butter or other fat, melted
1/3 cup salmon liquid
2/3 cup dry bread crumbs
2 eggs, beaten
¼ cup parsley, chopped
1 teaspoon powdered mustard
½ teaspoon salt
2 tablespoons butter
Lemon wedges

Drain salmon, reserving liquid. Flake salmon. Cook onion in butter until tender. Add salmon liquid, 1/3 cup bread crumbs, eggs, parsley, mustard, salt, and salmon. Mix well. Shape into 6 cakes and roll in remaining crumbs. Place cakes in a heavy frying pan which contains about ⅛ inch of fat, hot but not smoking. Fry at moderate heat. When cakes are brown on one side, turn carefully and brown the other side. Cooking time approximately 5 to 8 minutes. Drain on absorbent paper. Cut rolls in half. Spread with butter. Place cakes in rolls. Serve with lemon wedges. Makes six sandwiches.

TUNA-SALMON PATTIES

1 can (6½ ounces) tuna, drained
1 can (7¾ ounces) salmon, cleaned and drained
3 whole saltine crackers, crushed
1 egg
Salt and pepper to taste

Mix above ingredients well. Shape into 2-inch patties. Heat enough oil to cover bottom of frying pan. Fry patties over medium heat until brown on both sides, about 10 to 15 minutes. Makes 8 to 10 patties.

ORANGE-SALMON PATTIES

2 navel oranges
1 medium onion
1 can (15½ ounces) salmon
½ cup bread crumbs
2 teaspoons Worcestershire sauce
Salt and freshly ground black pepper to taste
2 tablespoons vegetable oil
Orange Sauce (recipe follows)

Peel and seed oranges and cut into small pieces. Chop onion medium-fine. Drain salmon. Combine all the ingredients except for the oil and mix well. Shape into 8 patties. Heat oil in large skillet. Saute patties in hot oil over medium heat until golden brown on one side. Turn and brown on second side. Serve with Orange Sauce.

Orange Sauce:
¾ cup plain yogurt
6 tablespoons frozen reconstituted orange juice

Combine ingredients and mix until smooth. Serve at room temperature or warmed slightly.

SALMON PATTIES

2 large eggs
2 cans (7¾ ounces each) salmon, drained and flaked
2/3 cup fine dry bread crumbs
1 medium onion (4 ounces), finely chopped (½ cup)
¼ cup parsley leaves, finely chopped (2 tablespoons)
1 to 2 tablespoons lemon juice
¼ teaspoon salt
Pepper to taste
1 cup corn oil (for shallow frying)

In a medium bowl, beat eggs enough to blend yolks and whites; stir in salmon, 1/3 cup of the bread crumbs, the onion, parsley, lemon juice, salt and pepper until well-mixed. Shape into four (each about 1 inch thick) oval-shaped patties. Coat with remaining 1/3 cup bread crumbs.

Line a tray with wax paper and place the patties, well apart, on it; refrigerate for at least 30 minutes.

In a 10-inch skillet over medium heat, heat oil. Add patties. Shallow-fry, turning once, until evenly browned. Drain on paper towels. Serve very hot. Good accompanied by tartar sauce. Serves four.

AK Enterprises Books

Please fill out this form and return to:

**AK Enterprises
P.O. Box 210241
Anchorage, Alaska 99521-0241**

Please send me _____ copies of
Alaska Shrimp and Crab Recipes .... $12.95 each

Please send me _____ copies of
Alaskan Halibut Recipes .... $12.95 each

Please send me _____ copies of
Salmon Recipes from Alaska .... $12.95 each

Please send me _____ copies of
Moose and Caribou Recipes from Alaska .... $12.95 each

Total amount for books: $_____

$1.00 per book for postage/handling $_____

Total amount enclosed: $_____

Send books to:

Name: _____

Address: _____

City: _____

State/Zip: _____

Thank you very much for your order. Good cooking!

ORDER FORM
AK Enterprises Books

Please fill out this form and return to:

**AK Enterprises
P.O. Box 210241
Anchorage, Alaska 99521-0241**

Please send me _____ copies of
Alaska Shrimp and Crab Recipes .... $12.95 each

Please send me _____ copies of
Alaskan Halibut Recipes .... $12.95 each

Please send me _____ copies of
Salmon Recipes from Alaska .... $12.95 each

Please send me _____ copies of
Moose and Caribou Recipes from Alaska .... $12.95 each

Total amount for books: $_____

$1.00 per book for postage/handling $_____

Total amount enclosed: $_____

Send books to:

Name: _____

Address: _____

City: _____

State/Zip: _____

Thank you very much for your order. Good cooking!